# WHAT DO THEY HEAR?

# WHAT DO THEY HEAR?
## BRIDGING THE GAP BETWEEN PULPIT & PEW

Mark Allan Powell

Abingdon Press
*Nashville*

**WHAT DO THEY HEAR?**
**BRIDGING THE GAP BETWEEN PULPIT AND PEW**

Library of Congress Cataloging-in-Publication Data

Powell, Mark Allan, 1953-
   What do they hear? : bridging the gap between pulpit and pew / Mark Allen Powell.
      p. cm.
   ISBN-13: 978-0-687-64205-2 (binding: adhesive, pbk., perfect : alk. paper)
   1. Preaching. 2. Bible—Homiletical use. 3. Bible—Reader-response criticism.  I. Title.

   BS534.5.P69  2007
   251—dc22

All scripture quotations unless noted otherwise are taken from the *New Revised Standard Version of the Bible,* copyright 1989, by the Division of Christian Education of the National Council of the Churches of Christ in the United States of America. Used by permission. All rights reserved.

The following scripture quotations are used with permission:

(KJV) from the King James or Authorized Version of the Bible.

(RSV) from the Revised Standard Version of the Bible, copyright 1946, 1952, 1971 by the Division of Christian Education of the National Council of the Churches of Christ in the United States of America.

(NASB) from the New American Standard Bible® © Copyright 1960, 1962, 1963, 1968, 1971, 1972, 1973, 1975, 1977, 1995 by The Lockman Foundation.

(NEB) from the New English Bible. © The Delegates of the Oxford University Press and The Syndics of the Cambridge University Press 1961, 1970.

(JB) from THE JERUSALEM BIBLE, copyright © 1966 by Darton, Longman & Todd, Ltd. and Doubleday, a division of Random House, Inc.

(NIV) from the HOLY BIBLE, NEW INTERNATIONAL VERSION®. NIV®. Copyright © 1973, 1978, 1984 by International Bible Society. Zondervan Publishing House. All rights reserved.

(NAB) from the New American Bible with Revised New Testament and Psalms Copyright © 1991, 1986, 1970 Confraternity of Christian Doctrine, Inc., Washington, DC. All rights reserved.

07 08 09 10 11 12 13 14 15 16—10 9 8 7 6 5 4 3 2 1

MANUFACTURED IN THE UNITED STATES OF AMERICA

Dedicated to

Charles Arthur Powell

my brother

# TABLE OF CONTENTS

# PREFACE

This book is for preachers. It offers reflection on experiments that I have done regarding how people understand stories. I am a literary critic, with specialization in
biblical studies. I am also a preacher. I initiated these
experiments to learn about literary criticism and in so
doing I learned a few things about the Bible. I also learned
some things that I think are relevant for preaching, which
I want to share with you now.

The experiment reported in chapter 2 of this book was
previously presented in one chapter of a *Festschrift* dedicated to Robert H. Tannehill. There, the results served as a
springboard for an exegetical study of Luke 15:11-32
(Parable of the Prodigal Son). Some of those results are
summarized here, but the main interest now is in what we
can learn from this experiment regarding the challenge
and promise of preaching the Word of God in diverse circumstances. Those who want to know what I said about the
parable itself (with implications for Lukan theology)
should consult the previous publication: "The Forgotten
Famine: Personal Responsibility in Luke's Parable of 'the
Prodigal Son' " in *Literary Encounters with the Reign of
God,* ed. Sharon H. Ringe and H. C. Paul Kim, 265–87 (New
York: T& T Clark, 2004).

The experiments discussed in chapters 3 and 4 were previously reported in one chapter of a book on biblical hermeneutics, which I still think just might be the best book I have ever written. It has an odd title and might not have reached everyone who would be interested in it. It lays out a workable exegetical method that transcends the interests of historical criticism (without, I hope, violating them): the goal is to develop an approach to biblical interpretation that allows texts to mean different things to different people without granting carte blanche for them to mean anything to anybody. The experiments reported in that book were conducted to explore the boundaries of multiple interpretation (polyvalence) and to illustrate the need for the method that is then presented in the pages that follow. Readers who would like to know more about this method may want to check out this volume: *Chasing the Eastern Star: Adventures in Biblical Reader-Response Criticism* (Louisville: Westminster John Knox, 2001).

So, I have previously reported on these experiments in academic tomes and settings, with a principal interest in biblical interpretation, hermeneutics, and epistemology. It was John Kutsko of Abingdon Press who heard one of my presentations at an academic conference and immediately saw the implications for preaching. He urged me to get this data out of the ivory towers and into the hands/heads/hearts of parish pastors. If you benefit from what is offered here, you have John and the good folks at Abingdon to thank. They have been a pleasure to work with, not least because of their unswerving and obvious devotion to serving Jesus Christ and the people he loves.

Also join me in thanking Trinity Lutheran Seminary, which grants me the time and resources to produce works such as this. They do so unselfishly, moved by the Spirit to be faithful servants of God and Christ's church.

# CHAPTER ONE

# FOR THOSE WHO HAVE
# EARS TO HEAR

When I was in high school, way back in 1969, my mother told me that she liked "that song on the radio about the bathroom." She didn't usually like Top 40 music, so I was intrigued—but I had no idea what song she was talking about. She explained: "The one that goes, 'There's a bathroom on the right!'" The song is "Bad Moon Rising," performed by Creedence Clearwater Revival, and the actual line is, "There's a bad moon on the rise." But lyrics had not been the primary attraction for Mom anyway—she just liked how it sounded.

A few years back some folks put together a series of books on misheard song lyrics—volumes with titles like *'Scuse Me While I Kiss This Guy* (Fireside, 1995) and *He's Got the Whole World in His Pants* (Fireside, 1996). People with apparently healthy eardrums received the same auditory signals as everyone else and yet *heard* something very different. What could account for such anomalies? Was it Freudian?

Most pastors and teachers—or public speakers in general—have experienced the phenomenon of being misheard in bizarre or eccentric ways. We had a student at the seminary not too long ago who wondered why the Bible professors kept talking about an "extra Jesus" (the word was *exegesis*). I could not help but recall Gilda Radner's character on 1970s episodes of *Saturday Night Live*—the feisty Emily Litella who would give rabid editorials objecting to something she had heard on the news only to discover that she'd completely misheard a significant word or phrase. Emily would go on about "the Eagle Rights amendment" or "violins on television" until someone explained the matter to her; then she'd look at the camera and say, "Never mind."

This book is about unanticipated interpretations of a different sort. If you have a problem with people misunderstanding the very words you utter, I have only obvious advice to offer: get a better sound system, learn to enunciate, use visual aids, be redundant. But many of us who preach and teach for a living have encountered a different kind of misunderstanding: people hear our words correctly but take them in ways we do not intend. They find implications we might not endorse and draw conclusions we might not recommend. We want to explain ourselves more fully: "When I said God works all things for the good, I wasn't suggesting God *wants* us to suffer" or "Daniel in the lion's den is a *somewhat* different context than corporate review panels." But, ultimately, this is a lost cause. We don't want to clutter our sermons with countless caveats, and it is not practical to follow people around offering further commentary whenever a potential for questionable application arises. We speak, and our audience decides what to do with our words—the listeners have the power not only to accept them or reject them but also to define them contextually, to decide what our words mean *to them* and *for them*. They do this, consciously or subconsciously, without our permission and, often, without our knowledge.

For them, our words serve simply as the stuff out of which meaning can be made.

Still, this is not always a problem, is it? Sometimes, the flexibility of interpretation works to our advantage. Most preachers discover that their sermons can have beneficial effects beyond anything they actually had in mind. People find relevance in our words for situations we knew nothing about, or they make connections that we might not have made ourselves but now recognize as appropriate. We are embarrassed to take credit for such surprises—we smile or wink and say, "It must have been the Holy Spirit."

Yes. I believe it *is* the Holy Spirit—but that does not necessarily mean there is anything supernatural going on. Communication theory can account for serendipity. Indeed, coincidences can be encouraged. We can learn to preach in ways that invite fortuitous application of our words: gnomic sayings, images, symbols, and anecdotes are pregnant with potential for polyvalence, and the more we employ them, the more likely our parishioners will be to pursue possibilities for meaning that stretch the parameters of our limited intent.

I come to this topic as one trained in literary criticism, where the just-mentioned polyvalence has been all the rage for more than a decade now. Simply put, *polyvalence* refers to the capacity—or, perhaps, the *inevitable tendency*—for texts to mean different things to different people. Literary critics differ drastically in their evaluation of polyvalence (i.e., friend or foe?), but virtually all literary critics now recognize the reality of this phenomenon: texts *do* mean different things to different people and at least some of the interpretive differences that have been examined (e.g., gender-biased interpretations) appear to follow fairly predictable patterns.

The potential for polyvalence may be a bane to authors of instruction manuals, medical prescriptions, or legal documents, but it is surely a boon to poets. Preachers and politicians fall somewhere in between: they depend upon a degree of ambiguity, but only a degree. Yes, we preachers share that hypocrisy with the politicians—for all our complaining about being "taken out of context," we want our words to achieve a greatness beyond what we instill in them. We want them to exceed our expectations, to accomplish purposes beyond our purview. Indeed, we want our words to accomplish the very purposes of God (Isa. 55:11), which by definition lie beyond anything discernible within the context of our own thoughts and ways (Isa. 55:8). Truth be known, we *want* to be taken out of context—but only when that is a good thing.

In any case, it seems inevitable. We want our sermons to be meaningful to people and for people, but we do not actually make that happen. Most of the time, our role is simply to provide people with the raw materials out of which they can make meaning for themselves. We provide the materials, but we are impotent to control the final assembly. We are fortunate if we even get to witness that construction, to inspect it when it is done.

Wouldn't it be great if we could *maximize* the possibility of our words finding widespread application in ways that meet our approval and *minimize* the possibility of them being taken in ways that don't meet our approval? Polyvalence within parameters—that would be perfect.

In my work as a literary critic, I have tried to distinguish between interpretations that are invited by the text (though not necessarily intended by the author) and interpretations that are not invited by the text (almost certainly not intended by the author). I have often used a simple example of four persons reading the story of Jesus' crucifixion in the Gospel of Matthew. They respond to the story in different ways:

Reader One is *inspired* by the story because it presents Jesus as a man of integrity who is willing to die nobly for his convictions.

Reader Two is *traumatized* by the story because it reveals the depth of human depravity on the part of those who denounce, betray, and torture an innocent man.

Reader Three is *comforted* by the story because it portrays Jesus' death as an atoning sacrifice through which God offers forgiveness to the undeserving.

Reader Four is *delighted* by the story because it reports the execution of a meddlesome busybody who tried to tell everyone else how to live.

The first three responses seem to be invited by the text—the fourth does not. The first three readings pick up on signals and nuances within the story, engaging it in variant ways. The fourth appears to defy the narrative's rhetoric in a way that avoids engaging the text but, rather, imposes a foreign perspective upon it. All four are examples of polyvalence, but only the first three exemplify polyvalence that lies within the parameters of meaning invited or envisioned by the narrative.

There are a couple of points here for preaching. First, let us note that the first three readings, while diverse, are not really competitive or contradictory. It would be a bit presumptuous for any one of these readers to insist that his or her response was the only "correct interpretation" of the story. It would also be difficult for us to ascertain exactly which of these three responses the author of Matthew's Gospel actually intended to evoke. Perhaps he intended only one of them—and would be (pleasantly?) surprised to discover that his story sometimes worked in other ways. Or perhaps he foresaw all three possibilities and hoped he would have readers who would respond in all these ways. We cannot know—he is unavailable for interview. What we can say is that the author of Matthew's Gospel provided readers with raw material appropriate for the creation of these three types of meaning. That, I think, corresponds to something we might want to do in our sermons.

But what about that fourth reader? This reader appears to have approached the story with values and perspectives radically different from those that the author assumed his readers would hold. That can happen with our sermons also: every communication must assume a certain "target audience," and hearers who do not fit the assumed paradigm may respond in unanticipated ways. Reader Four may seem like a fairly extreme example, but even the most homogenous congregation can include persons with diverse outlooks. Thus, it might be a useful exercise to identify the assumptions we make regarding the target audience for our sermons: what do we take for granted concerning the *point of view* of the community in which these sermons are heard? We might begin such an exercise by listing the values, beliefs, and commitments that seem to govern the lives of our parishioners. That's a good start, but *point of view* can encompass other things as well.

One time, I preached a sermon that was intended to arouse thanksgiving for the providence of God. I employed illustrations that called attention to the goodness of God that had been shed abroad in people's lives—the kind of "chicken soup for the soul" stories that are supposed to be effective at touching people's hearts. I touched hearts, but not always in the way I had anticipated. At that point in my ministry, I was regularly soliciting feedback (always a good idea) and some who had heard the sermon reported that they were aroused not to thanksgiving, but to envy and covetousness. This, obviously, had not been my intent. What went wrong? As it turns out, the effectiveness of my illustrations depended on the hearers being able to *empathize* with the recipients of bounty described in the stories I told. Some were able to do that, and their identification with persons who had been blessed by God fostered a sense of gratitude within them. But everything depended on that connection being made, and for others it just didn't happen. They heard me talking about good things that God does for some people—other people—and their gut-level response was to wonder why God didn't do things like that for them.

It would be easy to criticize these people: Why are they so selfish? Can't they just be grateful that God is good to anyone? Why does everything have to be about them? But this seems pointless. Lots of things would be easier if the people to whom we preach were better people . . . if they weren't such sinners! Meanwhile, I decided that I needed to learn a few things about empathy, and I discovered that literary critics know quite a bit about this subject. They have been studying empathy for a long time and they know about strategies storytellers sometimes use to encourage it. Such strategies might have made my sermon more effective. But, more to the point, literary critics know that empathy can never be forced. It should not be taken for granted. It is, in fact, one aspect of *point of view,* so assumptions about an audience's empathy choices are as significant as those about other matters of perspective (values, beliefs, or commitments). Bottom line: a sermon that assumes a particular point of empathy for its intended effect will only achieve that effect for those who make the connection; others may construct a meaning outside the parameters of the preacher's intent. And, since empathy cannot be controlled, a sermon that depends upon a particular empathy choice to achieve its intended effect will probably not succeed with everyone in the audience.

Literary criticism is attentive to different elements *within texts* that allow for "polyvalence within parameters," and literary criticism is also attentive to different factors *within readers* that account for responses that resist or defy what the text seems to invite. Indeed, the primary focus of literary criticism for the past two decades has been on bridging the gap between authorial intent and reader response. To the extent that sermons are "texts" (albeit oral ones), preachers may be able to learn a few things from literary critics that will help them to bridge the gap between pulpit and pew.

We want our sermons to be texts that lend themselves to multiple interpretation, but we don't want them to be texts that can just mean anything to anybody. We want to create texts that provide people with the raw materials for constructing a particular sort of meaning—and we know that some will do this better than others; some will do it more elaborately, some more intensely, some more permanently—but we hope that very few will use what we provide for the construction of meaning that is completely contrary to what we had in mind.

Ultimately we have no control over how people respond to our words. Recognizing that lack of control can be liberating as well as frightening, but it does not relieve us of responsibility for doing what we can. One thing we can do—and will do in this little book—is learn a few things about how and why texts mean different things to different people. And *specifically* we will learn a bit about how texts mean different things to clergy than they do to laity. We will be stereotyping, of course, and any number of exceptions to the generalities might intervene for particular cases and circumstances. But we will learn a few *basic* things about how clergy and laity make meaning out of texts.

Why? Sermons are usually texts about texts. Though a sermon may be an oral text in its own right, it is also often a reflection upon a written text, namely some passage from the Bible. Accordingly, different perceptions of meaning in a sermon may have a background in different perceptions of meaning in scripture. Few pastors will be surprised to hear that clergy and laity read scripture differently. Clergy have been trained to read scripture exegetically, to discover meaning in light of knowledge that laity lack and through the application of critical methods laity do not employ. Obviously, then, preachers will often find in scripture a meaning or sense that would not have been readily apparent to their parishioners. The point, then, is to draw upon that advanced understanding without letting it become a barrier that separates us from our listeners. A colleague of mine says that exegesis is like underwear: your congregation wants to be able to assume it is there, but they don't want you to show it to them.

I was privileged to spend a few days with gospel music legends Bill and Gloria Gaither in 2003. At the time I wasn't much of a fan of Southern gospel music (though I've since developed a bit more appreciation for the genre), but I was intrigued by their popularity. The American Society of Composers and Performers named the Gaithers "the most successful songwriters of the twentieth century" and declared that their songs have been performed and sung by more people than any other composers in history: more than George and Ira Gershwin, more than Rodgers and Hammerstein, more than Lennon and McCartney. What's the secret? Bill says they make a great team: Gloria is the intellectual, ethereal type, while he is the down-home country boy. Specifically, he says, "She keeps things theologically sound, while I keep asking, 'Can we put some of those cookies on the bottom shelf where everyone can reach?'" I recall seeing a cartoon in *Leadership* magazine many years ago that showed a preacher looming over his congregation and bellowing defensively, "Now some of you may think this smacks of Sabellianism . . ." This preacher was probably out of touch with the concerns of the average congregant.

Intellectual knowledge and specialized training present one sort of gap between pastors and their parishioners, but my guess is that most preachers are aware of this. You probably don't need a book to help you cross that divide, though you might need a nudge now and then to help you remember it exists. As suggested above, it may help to have some system for obtaining reliable feedback from representative members of the congregation. Still, in my experience, this is only one of many potential causes for a disconnect between pulpit and pew, and since it is relatively easy to detect and correct, it need not be our primary concern.

I want to share with you the results of a couple of experiments that I have conducted—instances in which I have actually compiled data concerning how clergy and laity responded to particular texts of scripture. I began conducting these experiments over a decade ago and on at least two occasions came up with results that I consider to be quite striking. Chapters 3 and 4 of this book present the results of two studies that I think you will find worthy of consideration. First, however, I want to provide some background material on the concept of "social location" and its implications for understanding the phenomenon of polyvalent interpretation. I realize that might not sound very interesting, but we will stay mostly in the practical realm (avoiding a morass of complicated theory), and before we are done I promise to give you some different perspectives on a text that you have probably preached so many times that you thought nothing new could possibly be said concerning it. I hope that promise will entice you to read chapter 2 now and not just skip to the main event—the stuff about clergy and laity—in the two chapters that follow. But I can only hope. I am just an author and I don't have any ultimate control over what you do with my words. Do I?

# Chapter Two

# Social Location: A Matter of Perspective

When literary critics talk about *social location*, they mean the complex of factors that can be used to distinguish groups of readers from other readers who differ from them in some respect. There are many factors on which such a distinction can be based: race, gender, age, nationality, economic class, political affiliation, and so forth. Thus, we might speak of "male readers" as distinct from "female readers" or of "young readers" as opposed to "middle-aged readers." Any actual human being is a complex of such factors—a "male reader" is not *just* male, but will be many other things as well (young, black, American, middle-class, heterosexual, Methodist, Republican, etc.).

For a long time now, literary critics have claimed that social location influences the interpretation of texts. Patterns of polyvalence can often be linked to such factors: "men" as a social group respond differently to stories than "women." Likewise, "*white* women" respond differently to stories than "*black* women." And "*American* black women" respond differently than "*African* black women." Tracing the ways in which social location affects the interpretation of stories gets complicated because any given reader is a complex of multiple factors, and there is no sure way of knowing which factor will prove to be most influential at any particular time. Even so, some general tendencies are evident because *communities* have stories that connect with texts: if you belong to the community of "males" or "Americans" or "Lutherans" or "clergy," you will probably be affected by stories in ways that are typical of those social groups. You will make subconscious connections between the story you are hearing and the story (experience) of being male or American or Lutheran or whatever.

This phenomenon has implications for the effectiveness of storytelling. If the goal of storytelling is to convey a particular message, that goal may only be accomplished for readers of a targeted social location. But a broader goal of storytelling may be to present a narrative so full of meaning that it can affect diverse people in different ways. In that case, the story may be equally (though differently) effective for readers whose social locations vary.

The question for preachers may be, what is our goal? If, indeed, we want to communicate a fairly specific message, we need to take into account the somewhat diverse social locations of our audience members: perhaps we can communicate the message in a way that appeals to those factors they all have in common (denominational heritage, nationality); we also might be more intentional about varying our language and illustrations with regard to factors where their social location is diverse (gender, age, marital status). On another level, though, we might want to consider whether communicating a specific moral or message should always be the goal. A sermon that succeeds at simply telling the "old, old story of Jesus and his love" might connect with everyone in meaningful ways, including (for some) ways that we would not have been in a position to anticipate.

To illustrate how social location influences interpretation, I want to use the well-known Parable of the Prodigal Son. I did an experiment with this parable involving seminary students in three different countries. Let me begin, however, by explaining how I got the idea. In my teaching, I sometimes employ an exercise that I learned from David Rhoads. Here is how the exercise is described in an appendix to his book, written with Joanna Dewey and Donald Michie, *Mark As Story: An Introduction to the Narrative of a Gospel,* 2nd ed. (Augsburg Fortress Press, 1999).

> (1) Pair off and both read/study the episode silently; (2) Both close books, then the first person recounts to the other what he or she read, as faithfully as possible; (3) Both now look at the episode and see what details were accurately remembered and what was omitted, added, or changed in telling.

In my classes, at least, this exercise sometimes allows students to notice aspects of the text that they have not noticed before. They also discover mental changes that they have inadvertently made in the text. For example, we once used the story of the sinful woman who washes Jesus' feet in Luke 7:36-50. Two students in the class quoted Jesus as telling this woman, "Your sins are forgiven. Go and sin no more." Actually, he says only, "Your sins are forgiven" (see verse 48). The words, "Go and sin no more" are not found anywhere in this story—those words come from a completely different story about Jesus and another sinful woman in a completely different Gospel (John 8:1-11). Two of my students had inadvertently taken the words from this other story and imported them into this one. And when this was pointed out to them, they were flabbergasted. Both were *certain* that they had just read those words in the text only a moment earlier.

Does it make any difference? Well, if we are serious about scripture, I think we should try to be accurate—and that involves disciplining ourselves with regard to the tricks our minds play on us. Theologically, I don't know if this specific anomaly would make much difference or not—but it might. Some scholars think that the woman in Luke 7:36-50 is a prostitute; if so, they assume that she is probably a slave, as were the great majority of prostitutes at this time. She had not chosen her occupation and she could not give it up—no ex-prostitutes are mentioned anywhere in the New Testament (and that includes Mary Magdalene, who is never identified as a prostitute except in later traditions and Hollywood movies). Accordingly, the words "Go and sin no more" would have been less appropriate in this context than in John 8, where they are addressed to an adulterer. If this is all true, then the story in Luke 7 is less about Jesus absolving a penitent of specific immoral actions than it is about Jesus promising divine mercy to a miserable person for whom life as God intends does not appear to be an option. If that is the case, the students who were mentally inserting the words "Go and sin no more" where they did not belong could have been reading the story in light of what was at best a tangential concern.

At any rate, I sometimes employ exercises like this just to get the students into the text and to see if anything worthy of discussion comes up. One time, we did this with regard to the Parable of the Prodigal Son in Luke 15:11-32. On that day, twelve seminary students read the text carefully, then recounted it from memory to twelve partners. Not one of them mentioned the famine to which Jesus refers in 15:14. They all retold the story in ways that went something like this: "The younger son asked his father for his share of the inheritance and he went off to a far country—but when he got there, he squandered all the money and pretty soon he was broke—so he got a job feeding pigs and was so hungry that he wished he could eat the pig food—then he realized . . ." The story in Luke's Gospel actually says that after the boy squandered his money, "a severe famine took place throughout that country, and he began to be in need" (15:14), but that must have seemed like such an extraneous detail that it simply dropped out of the memory banks for all twelve of my students that day. I must admit that I had also thought the famine reference was a pretty extraneous detail, but I was struck by the unanimity of the omission—*all* of them forgot the famine—and that prompted me to conduct a bit more research.

I organized a more controlled study involving one hundred students, only six of who would mention the famine in their oral recounting of Luke's tale. The famine-forgetters, furthermore, comprised students of diverse gender, race, age, economic status, and religious affiliation. No single factor of social location seemed to have any statistically relevant impact on the likelihood that a reader would or would not remember the famine after reading this parable.

Of course, all one hundred respondents were Americans. The next logical step, then, was to survey non-American readers, and I had the opportunity to do this when I spent a portion of 2001 on sabbatical in Eastern Europe. There, I polled diverse respondents in the city of St. Petersburg, Russia. I was only able to access a sample one-half the size of that in America (fifty total respondents as opposed to one hundred) but a shocking forty-two of these specifically mentioned the famine when they re-told the story that they had just been asked to read. Again, the likelihood of such recall could not be linked statistically to any specific factor(s) of social location within the St. Petersburg sample. The only factor that emerged as relevant in this survey was the geographical one: only six out of one hundred Americans remembered the famine, compared to forty-two out of fifty Russians.

One probably does not need to look too far for a social or psychological explanation for this data. In 1941, the German army laid siege to the city of St. Petersburg (then Leningrad) and subjected its inhabitants to what was in effect a 900-day famine. During that time, 670,000 people died of starvation and exposure—about one fourth of the total population. Some of the current inhabitants of the city are survivors of that horror; more are descendants of survivors. Other residents represent a new generation of immigrants, but even for these a collective memory remains strong in the cultural milieu. In modern St. Petersburg, typical social issues (abortion, care of the elderly, imprisonment of lawbreakers, socialized medicine, etc.) are often considered through the lens of an important question: *but what if there is not enough food?* And no one thinks it odd for university students to write papers on "The Ethics of Cannibalism." It is, I think, not surprising that in *this* social location, more than four-fifths of the people who read Luke's story of the prodigal son did not forget that there was a famine. To them, the mention of a famine is never an extraneous detail.

This is somewhat intriguing, but again we might wonder whether the famine actually adds a whole lot to the story. Would it make any difference in how we preach this text? This portion of the parable seems to have four key elements:

1. the young man acquires his inheritance prematurely
2. he squanders his property in a faraway land
3. a famine comes
4. he is left in dire straits.

In defense of the American students, it is logically possible to leave out the third step. The story stills make sense. Granted, the arrival of a famine may have exacerbated things or intensified the young man's plight, but if one leaves it out entirely, the story still makes sense.

Or, I should say, *a* story still makes sense. Consider this: the second step in the summary above might also be viewed as expendable—the famine alone could account for the boy's distress, even apart from any squandering. How interesting, then, that a good number of Russian readers made no mention of the boy squandering his property when they recounted this story. In fact, only seventeen of the fifty made mention of this point, which had been remembered by all of the Americans. To put that in percentages:

| Americans: 100 % mention squandering | 6 % mention famine |
|---|---|
| Russians: 34 % mention squandering | 84 % mention famine |

Basically, we have two different versions of the story that is told in Luke 15:13-14. The American students tended to tell that story according to what is printed in boldface type below:

**A few days later the younger son gathered all he had and traveled to a distant country, and there he squandered his property in dissolute living. When he had spent everything,** a severe famine took place throughout that country and **he began to be in need.**

This, as we have indicated, makes good sense—one might argue that the forgotten famine was but a superfluous detail that adds nothing essential to the story. But the Russian students tended to remember the story this way:

**A few days later the younger son gathered all he had and traveled to a distant country, and** there he squandered his property in dissolute living. When he had spent everything, **a severe famine took place throughout that country and he began to be in need.**

This also makes sense. Squandering the money becomes a minor, forgettable detail. The logic of the Russian students seemed to be the reverse of the Americans: a famine alone is sufficient to explain why a young man would end up hungry and in need; the fact that this man had previously squandered his property merely exacerbates the situation and intensifies his plight. I asked the Russian students about this in follow-up conversations. "So what if he lost his inheritance?" they responded. "That just means he would be poor like everyone else. Most people don't have an inheritance to lose. But when the famine came, *that* was a problem."

Now we are getting closer to matters that might be significant for preaching. I have not heard many American sermons that portray the prodigal as a famine victim— more often, the story is regarded as a paradigm for repentance: the boy "comes to himself" and determines to go home, telling his father, "I have sinned against heaven and against you!" (15:17-18). Perhaps, then, the famine gets ignored because it was not the boy's fault, and most sermons that I have heard on this text want to be clear that the boy's downfall was his own doing. He wasn't just a victim of bad luck—he went from riches to rags because of his own irresponsible behavior.

So, I tried that out on the Russian students: "Aren't we supposed to think that the boy did something wrong?" Of course, they told me. But the boy's mistake was not how he spent his money—or how he lost it. His mistake was leaving his father's house in the first place. His sin was placing a price tag on the value of his family, thinking that money was all he needed from them. Once he had his share of the family fortune, the family itself no longer mattered. In a phrase, his sin was *wanting to be self-sufficient*.

I told them about the American students, and this prompted further discussion: How revealing it is that Americans think the great sin was wasting money. They think this because money is very important to them. In a capitalist country, it must be a very bad thing to squander one's inheritance. But in a socialist state, the sin is self-sufficiency. This boy's sin was that he wanted to make it in the world on his own. He trusted in his finances and in his own sense of rugged individualism, and he figured that would be enough to get by. And, who knows, he might have made it if not for the famine. But that's what happens, Jesus says. Famines *do* come—and in a world where there are famines (and factory closings and automobile accidents and medical emergencies), only a fool would want to be alone.

Our point at present is not to challenge either take on this parable but to illustrate the determinative effect that social location can have on interpretation of texts. Obviously, the text of Luke 15 mentions both squandering and famine—but readers tend to prioritize one element over the other, often to the point of dropping the minor element from consideration altogether. They do this subconsciously and yet seem prepared to defend the selection when it is pointed out to them. Literary critics would say that readers create meaning for themselves by selectively sorting and organizing the data that the text provides. Readers always do this, often while remaining oblivious to what they themselves are bringing to the process, unaware that the sorting and organizing of data is influenced by particular factors of their own social location. People who hear our sermons do the same thing—they sort the auditory data, prioritizing, organizing, remembering, forgetting: they create a meaning that seems appropriate to them with little awareness of the extent to which their social location has influenced that process.

## Wicked or Foolish?

Before we move on, let me just note a few other tidbits about this prodigal son story and how it has been received in Western and Eastern cultures. In a nutshell, the younger son is typically portrayed as foolish in Eastern cultures and as wicked or immoral in Western ones.

1. *The parallel to Joseph*. Almost all commentaries on Luke 15 written by authors in Eastern countries note connections between the story and the tale of Joseph in Genesis 37–50: (a) sibling rivalry between a young son and older brother(s); (b) the young son ends up separated from his father in a far country; (c) the young son is regarded as dead by his father; (d) the father gives his young son a ring and a robe (as Pharaoh gives Joseph in Genesis 41:42); (e) the father embraces his son in a noticeable display of affection (as Joseph does his father in Genesis 46:29). And, of course, both stories contain a famine. Indeed, the prodigal in Jesus' parable is often regarded as an antitype of Joseph: he is not sold into slavery against his will but voluntarily abandons his father's home for another land; in the far country he goes from riches to rags instead of the reverse; at the end of the story he travels home to be welcomed by his father instead of staying put to welcome a father who travels to see him. And, most important: whereas Joseph is regarded as the wisest man in all Egypt because he prepares for the famine that comes upon the land, the son in this parable is the opposite of wise (i.e., foolish) because he does not foresee that a famine could come and does nothing to prepare for it.

Western interpreters are much less likely to notice these allusions to Genesis or to make much of them. Out of fifty-five Western commentaries that I surveyed, only five mentioned possible parallels to the Joseph story. Of these five, two neglected to make any reference to the famine in their lists of points the stories have in common. Indeed, they proffered the suggestion that the prodigal son is an antitype to Joseph because while Joseph resisted the allures of Potiphar's wife, the prodigal sought out prostitutes in the far country (more on that in a moment). Thus, Western commentators have not generally understood this parable by way of comparison with the Genesis tale, and even when they have done so, they have found the point of contrast to be not wisdom vs. foolishness but righteousness vs. immorality.

2. *Translation of a key word.* In Luke 15:13, the NRSV says that the young son "squandered his property in *dissolute* living." The Greek word that is translated *dissolute* in this verse is *asōtōs,* which can have two basic meanings. In a literal sense, the word simply means *wasteful*—it denotes the opposite of a commitment to "saving." But the word may also be used in a more figurative sense to mean *unhealthy*—it then denotes the opposite of a commitment to what is "salvific." Thus, Luke 15:13 might be taken literally to mean simply that the boy wasted his money instead of saving it: *how* he wasted it (what he spent his money on) would then be irrelevant. Or, Luke 15:13 might be taken more figuratively to mean that the boy spent his money in ways that were not salutary, i.e., on things that were not good for him and that might even be deemed wicked or immoral. By translating the word *dissolute,* the NRSV clearly favors the latter option, as do most English translations: "riotous living" (KJV); "a life of dissipation" (NAB); "loose living" (RSV, NASB); "reckless living" (NEB); "a life of debauchery" (JB); "wild living" (NIV). So it is intriguing to note what a representative of Eastern scholarship, Kenneth E. Bailey, says about this verse: "With only one exception, our Syriac and Arabic versions for 1800 years have consistently translated *asōtōs* as 'expensive' or 'luxurious' or 'spendthrift living'—with no hint of immorality" (see *Finding the Lost: Cultural Keys to Luke 15,* [Concordia Publishing House, 1992], 123). The Eastern Bible translations take *asōtōs* in its literal sense and present the young son as simply wasteful. This, of course, supports a reading of the story that views him as more "foolish" than "wicked."

3. *The older brother's assessment.* A similar tendency to that just noted can be observed with regard to what interpreters make of the older brother's comment in 15:30. The younger son has returned home to be welcomed by the father; the brother protests this and refers to the returnee as "this son of yours . . . who has devoured your property with prostitutes." Prostitutes? Is *that* what the boy spent

his money on? Western interpreters tend to think so—on this point, at least, they regard the older brother's testimony as reliable. Eastern interpreters, virtually without exception, regard the older brother's remark as a slanderous and probably baseless accusation. This affects how Luke 15:13 is understood. Here are a few sample quotes from what Bible commentaries say about that verse, regarding what the younger son did in the far country:

| Western Commentaries | Eastern Commentaries |
| --- | --- |
| 1. "The prodigal wastes his inheritance on sexual misconduct." | 1. "He was enamored of a love of luxury and splendor." |
| 2. "He went the whole route in sinful indulgence." | 2. "The boy wasted his possessions living luxuriously." |
| 3. "He wasted his money on 'wine, women, and song.'" | 3. "He pursued a life full of entertainment and amusement." |
| 4. "He goes abroad and lives a sinful life." | 4. "He was trouble-free." |

The authors of the Western commentaries appear to be interpreting Luke 15:13 in light of what the older brother says later (in 15:30), and they appear to assume that the brother's accusation is accurate. The authors of the Eastern commentaries make no such assumption and simply present the boy as spending his money on things that would not necessarily be immoral but that revealed no thought for the future. Thus, again: in the West, the boy is wicked; in the East, he is merely foolish.

## Bridging the Gaps

Literary critics speak of *gaps* that always occur in stories and create opportunity for polyvalent interpretation—ambiguous words, missing details, alternative perspectives, and other matters that even careful readers might construe in various ways. We have cited four gaps in the Parable of the Prodigal Son (there would be more):

1. The plight of the young man in the far country is attributed both to his own squandering and to a famine that comes upon the land—readers might emphasize either of these factors over the other.

2. The story contains possible parallels to the story of Joseph in Genesis—readers may or may not notice these and interpret the story in light of comparisons or contrasts to that separate narrative.

3. A key line in the story (15:13) uses the word *asōtōs,* which has both literal and figurative meanings—readers (of the Greek text) might take the word in either sense, as meaning literally "wasteful," or figuratively "unhealthy."

4. The story places an allegation regarding the boy's behavior on the lips of his older brother (15:30)—readers may take that comment as reliable or as slanderous.

What is interesting for our purposes is that readers have tended to resolve these gaps in ways that correspond with particular social locations. Western readers have been more likely to prioritize squandering over famine, to ignore allusions to Genesis, to take *asōtōs* figuratively, and to accept the older brother's allegation as valid. Taken together these decisions lead them to regard the story as a quintessential tale of moral repentance, a story that depicts sin as personal irresponsibility, illustrates the consequences of such sin, and then locates the key to redemption in an individual decision to reverse one's course through humble confession and capitulation to the authority against which one formerly rebelled. Eastern readers, by contrast, have tended to give more attention to the famine, to read the story as antithetical to the biblical narrative of Joseph, to take *asōtōs* in the literal sense of "wasteful," and to disregard the brother's comment as irresponsible slander. Those decisions lead them to regard the story as a tale of divine rescue: it is a story that depicts independence as a foolish choice (given the vicissitudes of life), and it is a story that locates redemption in the safe haven that God provides via family and community.

To put the matter differently, both Western and Eastern readers have viewed this as a story of conversion or transformation, but they appear to have construed that differently. At the risk of simplification, we might say that for Western readers the overall accent has been on *reform*, while for Eastern readers it has been on *recovery*. As I talked with the students from both America and Russia, various points and counterpoints were made that seemed to support either reading.

Point: The Americans told me that the climax of the story comes with the boy's decision to make a change and with the action he takes in light of that decision. The boy does not just sit in the pigpen waiting for someone to come and rescue him. Luke says, "he came to himself" (15:17) and then "he set off and went to his father" (15:20). If he had not done that, nothing would have changed—so the accent is on *reform*.

Counterpoint: The Russian students respond, Look at what the father says about that reunion. He says, "This son of mine was dead and is alive; he was lost and is found!" (15:24). He does not say, "he came back" (emphasizing what the son did) but says the boy *has been found*. And, again, he does not tell his other son, "We had to throw a party to celebrate your brother 'coming to himself' or 'deciding to come back home.' " He says, "We had to celebrate and rejoice because this brother of yours . . . was lost and *has been found*" (15:32). For the father in this story, the accent is on *recovery*.

Point: The American students told me that we need to look at this story in its context. The verse that comes immediately before the parable says, "There is joy in the presence of the angels of God over one sinner who repents" (15:10). In fact, this parable is the last in a series of three stories (lost sheep, lost coin, lost son) and Jesus explicitly says that the first two stories are about "a sinner who repents" (15:7, 10). Surely, we are supposed to believe the same is true for this one: it is about a sinner who repents (not just someone who gets rescued from a treacherous world). Thus, *reform*.

Counterpoint: The Russians students said, So look at the first two parables. Is the first one (15:3-7) about a bad sheep who learned its lesson about running away and is sure to stay with the flock from now on? Or is the second one (15:8-10) about a coin that got lost because of its inadequacies, compared perhaps to brighter, shinier coins? No. In both cases, the point is simply that what was lost (for whatever reason) was found and that this was a cause for joy. There is no mention of reform with regard to the sheep or the coin, so that should not be made prominent in the third story either. In all three cases, something that was lost was retrieved. Thus, *recovery*.

We could go back and forth like this all day, but what is the significance for preachers? If you are a Western preacher in a Western congregation, you probably don't have to worry too much about how your parishioners will resolve the kinds of issues that the story leaves ambiguous or open to interpretation. Most people in most of our churches will resolve those matters the same way we do— and studies such as this one serve only as interesting sidebars, prompting us to realize the benefit of sharing insights with those who read from perspectives other than our own.

But what would happen if you were a Western preacher in an Eastern congregation? If you resolved all four of the gaps mentioned above in the typical Western fashion, then there would be a gap of a different kind: a gap between pulpit and pew, which is the official subject of this book. Your assumptions about what seemed to be self-evident might not jibe with assumptions that seemed equally self-evident to your audience. Of course, if you really want to become a Western preacher to Eastern congregations, you will probably need a lot more help than this book can provide. But we are proceeding by way of analogy: right now, in the congregation you currently serve, there may be gaps of a less noticeable kind. The distinction between "clergy" and "laity" may not seem as dramatic as that between "Americans" and "Russians" or between "Westerners" and "Easterners," but it is a distinction nonetheless. Anytime "clergy" address "laity" there is a divide between two social locations, each of which processes the data of texts in distinctive ways.

## Postscript

Before we move on, allow me an epilogue to the prodigal son study. I had the opportunity to spend some time in Tanzania (East Africa) and I was curious to know whether the seminary students there would be more like the Russians or more like the Americans. I wanted to do another experiment—get fifty or one hundred of them to repeat the story from memory and note what they included and what they left out. I didn't have the opportunity for that, so I tried the next best thing: I gathered as many Tanzanian seminarians into a room as possible (about fifty) and told them I was going to read the story out loud to them and ask them to write down an answer to one question. I did that—read the whole story—and then asked, "Why does the young man end up starving in the pigpen?" I was curious to see how many would write "Because he wasted his money" and how many would write "Because there was a famine." A few did write responses like that, but the vast majority—around 80 percent wrote something completely different: "Because no one gave him anything to eat."

That wasn't even an option! That wasn't one of the two possible answers I had in mind. But if you check out the story in Luke 15, it does say that. It says, "he squandered his property" in verse 13, and it says, "a severe famine took place throughout the country" in verse 14, and it says, "no one gave him anything" in verse 16. Obviously, all three reasons contributed to why the young man ended up starving in the pigpen. So why were the Tanzanians struck by *this* reason, more than by the other two? Surely, they didn't think this was *central* to what the story was about, did they? Actually, they did.

I pressed the matter with them. I asked, "Why *should* anyone give him anything? Wasn't it his own fault—squandering his money like he did?" They told me this was a very callous perspective. The boy was in a far country. Immigrants often lose their money. They don't know how things work—they might spend all their money when they shouldn't because they don't know about the famines that come. People think they are fools just because they don't know how to live in that country. But the Bible commands us to care for the stranger and alien in our midst. It is a lack of hospitality not to do so. This story, the Tanzanians told me, is less about personal repentance than it is about society. Specifically, it is about the kingdom of God. It contrasts the father's house with the far country. The father's house is the kingdom of God that Jesus keeps talking about, but the far country is a society without honor. Everyone who heard this parable would be shocked by his depiction of such a society, a country that would let a stranger go hungry and not give him anything to eat. And a central point of the parable is that the scribes and the Pharisees are like that. Jesus tells the parable as a response to the scribes and Pharisees, who are grumbling that he welcomes sinners and eats with them (15:2). The parable teaches that the kingdom of God is a society that welcomes the undeserving, and it puts the scribes and Pharisees to shame by showing them that they are like a society with no honor, that shows no hospitality to the stranger in its midst.

# CHAPTER THREE

# EMPATHY CHOICES:
# CASTING THE SCRIPTURES

Stories appeal to our imagination. We have probably all had the experience of being so caught up in a story that we could easily imagine being there, in the story world among the characters. A friend of mine says that when she read J. R. R. Tolkien's *Lord of the Rings* as a teenager, she felt compelled to pray for Frodo and his company as though they were people she knew in the real world. She was genuinely worried about them and whether they would overcome their trials. Literary critics call such an effect *empathy*—an involuntary projection that causes us to identify with one or more of the characters in a story and experience the narrative in ways determined by that identification. The identification need not be so extreme as my friend's fixation with hobbits, but some degree of empathy is usually essential for a story to be effective or satisfying. Empathy is what enables us to cry at sad stories and tremble at scary ones. In a muted sense, we feel what we would feel if the story were real and we were experiencing it as the characters do.

In my own work on this subject, I have proposed a distinction between *realistic empathy* and *idealistic empathy*. The first is based on analogy and the second on fantasy. Truth be known, I am not really very much like James Bond or Spider-Man, but I always imagine I am when I watch those movies. And it's not just a gender thing—when I watched *Alias* (recent TV hit) I experienced the story as if I were Jennifer Garner (uh, make that Sydney Bristow, the character she played). I guess there must be something in me—something a therapist could ferret out—that makes me prefer being the person who saves the world to being the one who keeps needing to be rescued. I was always Underdog not Polly Purebred, Superman not Lois Lane (or, give me a break, Jimmy Olsen). At least I don't empathize with the villains (well, not usually). Still, there are times when I am drawn to a character I would not emulate, whom I have no desire to be like. Typically, this is due to some similarity, even a superficial one, that makes for a connection on a *realistic* level: like it or not, I really do have something in common with this character. So, even if it's Rev. Timothy Lovejoy in *The Simpsons* TV show or Elmer Gantry in the Sinclair Lewis novel, I can't help but feel an initial connection to any ordained minister in a tale. After all, I am one.

Thus, choice of empathy may be based on any number of factors, but such choices are usually made without awareness. Readers do not always realize that they have chosen to experience the story by identifying with certain characters rather than with other ones. Typically, they do not even consider the possibility of experiencing the story from alternative points of view—until, perhaps, they share notes with other readers who have done that. I think there must have been a whole generation of viewers who enjoyed traditional "cowboy and Indian" movies in a way that few people would today. Hollywood turned out dozens of films celebrating the exploits of brave men who conquered the western frontier by triumphing over hostile savages.

These films seemed to assume that their audiences would identify with the heroic cowboys and find the stories to be inspirational. Apparently, many people did experience them that way. Today, however, many viewers would be prone to regard such films as reflecting on a disgraceful aspect of American history. Why? Because they would empathize with the plight of the Native Americans in the stories and evaluate what is happening from *their* perspective. We might attribute this shift in perception to a variety of factors (e.g., changes in the social conscience), but my guess is that the original audiences (much less the film makers) did not anticipate that such a shift in empathy choice was even a possibility (or, at least, not a likelihood). Fans of these films did not consciously choose to identify with the cowboys as the "good guys" in these movies—they just did so with little awareness that anyone could ever experience the stories differently.

Empathy choices often align with factors of social location, but such choices may be impossible to predict for any given individual. Every individual is a complex of such factors. No one is *just* male or female; *just* white or black; *just* clergy or lay. So it can be interesting to become more cognizant of the empathy choices we make and of what these reveal about us. Does one factor trump all others? A man who always empathizes with male characters no matter what should realize that gender looms exceptionally large as a factor in his personal identity. A woman who always empathizes with idealistic figures over realistic ones just might be exceptionally ambitious or imaginative. We tend to make such choices subconsciously, but becoming more aware of them can enhance our self-understanding.

## The Good Samaritan

In our last chapter I related how social location affects interpretation of Luke's story of the Prodigal Son in Luke

15:11-32. I have had a similar experience with another one of the most popular parables in Luke's Gospel—the story of the Good Samaritan in Luke 10:30-37. I have heard many meditations on this tale over the decades, and the general consensus has always been that "the moral of the story" is that we ought to be willing to help anyone in need.

Indeed, I think that this understanding of the story is ingrained within our culture at a popular level that transcends churches or Bible study groups. Dartmouth College has a provision in their student handbook that allows students to inform campus security of a drunk student without fear of disciplinary action for either party. This provision is officially referred to as the school's Good Samaritan Policy. Likewise, in 1998, the television series *Seinfeld* closed out its nine-year run with an episode that had the main characters put on trial for violating a "Good Samaritan Law" in a small town they were visiting. The actual institution of such laws in some communities had been treated as a novelty news story by major networks prior to this episode, making them ripe for satirizing. But a few years later, Good Samaritan laws would receive mainstream attention in a more serious vein when French photographers were charged with not coming to the aid of Princess Diana after her fatal car crash. In fact, many European countries do have laws that require a person to summon aid or to help someone in an emergency when it is reasonably possible for them to do so; in America, such laws have been enacted by some states, but not by others, and they remain a matter of judicial controversy. But everywhere that such laws have been proposed or passed, they are known as "Good Samaritan laws," implying that people throughout Europe and America not only know the story of the "Good Samaritan" but also recognize the point of that story as being to motivate people to help those who are in need.

For the story to work in this way, the reader must be brought to a point of empathy with the Samaritan who stops to help the man in need. Preachers may simply exhort their congregants to make such an identification; poets may prefer the subtlety of rhetorical questions. In 1975, one of the most popular Christian folk songs in America was a number by Paul Clark called "Which One Are You?" In his three-stanza song, Clark allows his listener three options for empathy choice, but the correct choice is obvious: we should be like the Samaritan, not the priest or the Levite.

What we are really talking about here is *idealistic* empathy. The original Jewish audience for the story would have had more in common with the priest or the Levite than with the Samaritan, but the rhetoric of the story encouraged them to let idealistic empathy trump the more realistic bases for identification. When this happens, the reader discovers—almost unwittingly—that the idealistic bond may be preferable to connections based on other factors of social location. Preachers and poets have both realized that this is how the story works—or, at least, how it can work. Here are two examples from popular culture:

*The Cotton-Patch Version.* Clarence Jordan is remembered today as one of the founders of the model for Habitat for Humanity. In the sixties, he was a popular preacher and storyteller in Americus, Georgia. He liked to re-fashion Bible stories for modern times and tell them over the radio with a warm Southern drawl. Several of these were printed in books and issued on tapes and records as "cotton patch versions" of the scriptures. Jordan's version of the Good Samaritan may have been his best-known piece. In his telling of the tale, a man is beaten up by a gang of ruffians who hijack his car and leave him for dead. A revival preacher and then a gospel singer drive by but don't stop. Then, a black man stops to help the poor fellow. Jordan told this story so as to force his audience to identify with this third party. His rhetorical skill was such that he drew his white audience members in, and before they realized what was happening, he had them empathizing idealistically with a black man. This might not seem radical today—but it was enough to earn Jordan death threats at the time.

*A country-blues song.* Country singer Tom Stipe is now pastor of a church in Denver, Colorado. His 1991 album *Never Too Late* (Bluestone) ranks among the best country projects of its decade (in my humble opinion). But long before that, way back in 1973, Stipe recorded a country-blues tune called "Big City Blues" for a compilation album released by Maranatha! Music (called simply *Maranatha 3*). The song retold the story of the Good Samaritan in an urban setting. A guy named Willie comes to the city and "He was strollin' down First Avenue / Who do you think he run into? / Some boys lookin' for some fast cash / They knocked Willie in the head / Split with all his hard-earned bread / Tossed him in the alley with a crash." Of course, Willie gets ignored by various passersby—including institutional preacher-types. Then, a hippie "Jesus freak" happens by and fixes him up. Again, the song might sound dated today—but in 1973, hippie Jesus freaks were not preferred empathy choices for members of mainline churches or fans of country music.

In both of these cases, the retelling of the Good Samaritan story seems to assume an audience that would be likely to empathize realistically with the characters who fit the role of the "priest" or the "Levite" in the tale. The goal, then, is to motivate that audience to empathize idealistically with the "Samaritan" instead. The effectiveness of the retellings could probably be measured in terms of whether they accomplished this goal or not. They pose the question "Which one of these are you?" and propose the answer, "You may be the priest or the Levite, but you should be—and you can be—the Samaritan!"

How would you preach this story today? Who would the Samaritan be in your retelling of the story? An Arab? A Moslem? An AIDS patient? A homosexual? Can you imagine using this story to move your congregation toward unwitting empathy with those they may be likely to despise? My guess is that you *can* imagine doing that. The details may vary but most people in our culture recognize that this is what the Parable of the Good Samaritan is about: our commitment to ending human suffering ought to transcend political, ethnic, and other sorts of rivalries. The story asks the question, "Who is my neighbor?" and answers, "Anyone who needs my help."

I was a little surprised, therefore, to discover that many people around the world do not hear the story this way. When I lived in Tanzania, I found that very few people thought that this was the meaning of the story— or, at least, they did not think this was central to what the story taught us. The moral of the story, they told me, is that people who have been beaten, robbed, and left for dead cannot afford the luxury of prejudice. They will (and should) accept help from whoever offers it. Indeed, the *main* point of the story is that God helps us in unexpected and surprising ways. Therefore, when grain is brought to a famished village, parents of starving children should not care whether it is the Moslems or the Roman Catholics or the Jehovah's Witnesses who bring it. God can work through anyone, including those we might regard as heretics and apostates (which is how Jews would have viewed Samaritans). To the extent that the story raises the question, "Who is my neighbor?" the answer it provides is not "Whoever needs my help," but "Whoever helps me."

As in America, this understanding of the story has become part of the social culture, understood in secular circles and enacted at a political level. I learned that the Tanzanian government has a "Good Samaritan policy" in place, and this piqued my interest because I was aware that the U. S. government has such a policy as well. But in the United States, the Good Samaritan policy governs the bestowal of foreign aid—it allows us to provide disaster relief to other nations even when those countries are not considered to be our allies or friends. In Tanzania, the

Good Samaritan policy offers a statement of nonalignment with regard to receiving foreign aid—it was officially enacted to allow the country to accept aid from capitalist and communist governments without prejudice toward either. Under the Good Samaritan policy, Tanzania can essentially say, "We accept the help you offer, with gratitude, but this does not mean that we want to be like you or believe what you believe." That *is* one point to the parable: the man who is helped by the Samaritan is under no obligation to become a Samaritan himself.

The basic explanation for this different reading of the story is empathy choice. Americans tend to identify with the men walking down the road who must ask whether the person in the ditch is their neighbor. Tanzanians tend to identify with the person in the ditch and consider the question "Who is my neighbor?" from his perspective. Notably, that was not even one of the options provided in Paul Clark's folk song (page 33): Which one of these are you? Priest? Levite? Samaritan? The Tanzanian response, "None of the above—I am the person in the ditch" comes as a completely unanticipated option. It puts a different slant on the story—just how different we will see momentarily.

As I have shared this illustration in the United States, I have found that many Americans smile at this quaint understanding of a favorite tale. Obviously, the poor Tanzanians are prompted to hear the story this way because they have been needy all their lives. They don't often have the opportunity of helping others so must hear stories like this in terms of how others provide help for them. Well, that is one possibility. But it is also possible that they have just understood the story in the way that it was intended to work while our resistance to identifying with characters who are "needy" has caused us to miss out. In Luke's Gospel, Jesus does not ask the lawyer to whom he tells this parable, "Which of the three men regarded the person in the ditch as his neighbor?" He asks (in effect), "Which of the three would have been regarded as neighbor by the person in the ditch?" (see Luke 10:36). In short, Jesus challenges his audience (the lawyer) to identify not with any of the three persons who walked down the road (not realistically with the priest or Levite or idealistically with the Samaritan) but with the person in the ditch. He explicitly *requests* his audience to empathize with the person in the ditch—which is what the Tanzanians have done.

That is the main point of the story, they told me. The parable is not intended simply to present a moral tale about how people should be willing to help each other—that would be rather bland and obvious, and it seems unlikely that Jesus would have gotten crucified just for encouraging Jews and Samaritans to help each other. Rather, the main point of the story is that religious leaders (and by implication all religious people) need to evaluate their faith and life from the perspective of the most marginalized and vulnerable people of the earth. As Luke relates this story, a man who is some kind of religious scholar asks Jesus a theological question, "Who is my neighbor?" This was the sort of question that first-century religious scholars debated in first-century ivory towers. Who is my neighbor? Only Jews? Only Torah-observant Jews? Only Jews who belong to our particular sect or party? Various answers could be given, but Jesus does not even enter the debate. Instead of answering the question, he suggests a different way of asking it: what if you were beaten up, robbed, and left lying naked and half-dead in a ditch? *Then* how would you answer? The main point of this parable, the Tanzanians told me, is not to provide an orthodox answer to one particular question, but to propose an orientation for the consideration of all questions. Jesus suggests that we view the suffering people of the earth not just as "less fortunates" in need of our help, but as teachers whose perspectives and experiences reveal truth that power and privilege obscure.

From the Tanzanian perspective, identifying with the man in the ditch is not simply a quaint byproduct of their social location, but a faithful response to Christ. The Tanzanians would say, Jesus calls us all (Africans and Americans alike) to empathize with the powerless. Perhaps we do so more easily than you, but not to do so in *this* case is to miss the main point of the story.

Actually, I do not want to promote one way of reading this story over another. I've heard plenty of sermons on the Good Samaritan parable from different perspectives and on different continents. It is a polyvalent parable that provides readers in different settings with opportunities to construct meaning appropriate to their contexts. I trust the Holy Spirit to guide those processes. Nevertheless, as one who grew up understanding the Good Samaritan story one way, I did find it enlightening to hear an alternative take on a familiar tale. So, I hope we can take two things with us from this discussion: an awareness of how our subconscious empathy choices affect our experience of stories and an appreciation for how alternative choices can open stories to levels of meaning we might otherwise miss.

## Mark 7:1-8: Eating with Defiled Hands

Now we are going to move to an examination of social location that might hit a bit closer to home. I constructed a variety of experiments to test the manner in which clergy and laity understand the Bible. This one concerns a particular text of scripture, Mark 7:1-8.

Here is what I did: I gave fifty clergy a sheet of paper on which the text of Mark 7:1-8 (New Revised Standard Version) was printed, along with the question: "What does this story mean to you?" See page 40 for a sample of this sheet. Each pastor or priest was asked to read the text and answer the question. No one had access to commentaries or study aids that might influence his or her perception. I also made it clear that the answers would not be evaluated or shared in any way that would have names attached to them. Thus, I did my best to obtain honest responses that reflected genuine personal readings of the story, as opposed to studied responses that might reflect what the individual would want to say publicly. Then, I did the same thing with fifty laypersons.

I tried for diversity in both the clergy and lay samples—diversity of age, race, gender, marital status, economic class, and denominational background. I also managed to keep the ratios for such factors the same in both groups—the same number of women among the clergy as among the laity, the same number of African Americans, the same number of Roman Catholics, and so forth. It would have been impossible for me to control all factors of social location, but by and large, the two groups of people were remarkably similar except that one group consisted of fifty diverse clergy persons and the other of fifty diverse laypersons.

So, I ended up with one hundred answers to the question, "What does this story mean to you?" and I have printed all of these on the pages that follow. You may want to browse these now before continuing with my analysis of the comments. There are many interesting points that I do not address. I should indicate, however, that my numbering of the responses is not entirely random. They could have been presented in any order, but I tended to group together items that I found to be similar. Don't let those schemes override your own perceptions—especially on a first read. There would be many other patterns that a different order of presentation might bring to the fore. So, skim the lists and see if you can detect points of continuity or discontinuity:

Look *just* within the clergy sample (pages 40–45) to see if similar points keep being made—what are the main concerns or issues that keep coming up?

Look *just* within the lay sample (pages 45–50) for the same purpose—do similar points keep being made? What are the main concerns or issues that come up?

## Mark 7:1-8: What Does This Story Mean to You?

Now when the Pharisees and some of the scribes who had come from Jerusalem gathered around [Jesus], they noticed that some of his disciples were eating with defiled hands, that is, without washing them. (For the Pharisees, and all the Jews, do not eat unless they thoroughly wash their hands, thus observing the tradition of the elders; and they do not eat anything from the market unless they wash it; and there are also many other traditions that they observe, the washing of cups, pots, and bronze kettles.) So the Pharisees and the scribes asked him, "Why do your disciples not live according to the tradition of the elders, but eat with defiled hands?" He said to them, "Isaiah prophesied rightly about you hypocrites, as it is written, 'This people honors me with their lips, but their hearts are far from me; in vain do they worship me, teaching human precepts as doctrines.' You abandon the commandment of God and hold to human tradition."

### CLERGY RESPONSES

*Mark 7:1-8 Eating with Defiled Hands*

C-1. The folks in my church always say, "We've never done it that way before." Jesus wants me to tell them, "Human traditions are less important than God's commandments."

C-2. Scripture is more important than human traditions. People don't want to hear that, but it's true (and it's my job to tell them).

C-3. I need to be a prophet of mercy, not judgment. People hear enough condemnation already. Jesus affirms those who the world calls "unclean."

C-4. Jesus attacks the hypocrisy of religious legalism and expects us to do so as well.

C-5. If I want to be a faithful servant or a good pastor, I need to do what Jesus did: (a) denounce hypocrisy; (b) insist on true worship (from the heart); (c) teach divine commandments not human precepts.

C-6. The disciples are my church. The Pharisees are the world, the flesh, and the devil. My job is to build the faith of those the Lord has entrusted to my care and defend them from the accusations these enemies bring against them.

C-7. Traditions are from men, not God. True disciples trust in the Word, not traditions. The Lord has called me as a minister of his Word to make disciples by teaching his commandments. Sometimes this means exposing the hypocrisy of those whose hearts are not right with God.

C-8. I recognize these Pharisees—I think they joined my congregation! They worship with their lips and argue about things that are only "human"—precepts or traditions. I'm not going to thunder at them the way Jesus might ("You hypocrites!"), but I do hope I can get through to them in time.

C-9. I can easily relate to what Jesus faces here. The supposed inadequacies of his disciples are an implicit criticism of him. That's like saying I'm a bad pastor if the people in my church are sinners. If they weren't sinners, they wouldn't need me.

C-10. Jesus is able to recognize the hypocrisy of those who abandon God's Word because he knows the scriptures himself. I need to know the Word, memorize it, and live in it if I am to know what is of God as Jesus did.

C-11. Evil comes in many guises, as an angel of light, or here, in the form of those who worship with their lips and seem to be concerned about pious behavior. Jesus sees through their hypocrisy and exposes it. Lord, help me do the same.

C-12. Am I ready to do what Jesus did? Defend the guiltless and accuse the powerful? Comfort the afflicted and afflict the comfortable? That is the question the story raises for me.

C-13. How many of us have churches filled with people who worship with their lips but not their hearts? Ouch. That verse stings. But here, too, is the only solution. Teach "as doctrine" the Word of the gospel—not just self-help psychobabble—and you may reach a few.

C-14. I heard it said once that "nothing touches the heart but what comes from the heart." If I am right with God myself, then I can preach his Word as Jesus did and touch the hearts of those who have lost their way.

C-15. To *me*? To *me* the story says, if you want to be like Jesus, you need to be able to take the heat. Jesus isn't afraid to tell it like it is, even if that means knocking a few cherished traditions.

C-16. There is a real difference here between being religious and knowing God. I know that difference because I used to be "just religious" myself. Now that I am a pastor, people think I am a religious person, but my whole job as a pastor is to get religious people to see what a relationship with God is really all about. That is exactly what Jesus is doing here.

C-17. Jesus clarifies the true role of tradition. If it is to be more than empty ritual, people need to see how it is grounded in scripture and expressive of the heart. If we show people this, they will experience the liturgy (and other traditions) as something that draws them closer to God rather than as an obstacle to be overcome.

C-18. Any minister who is worth his or her salt must be prepared to confront hypocritical dependence on tradition ("the way we've always done it") when that conflicts with the leading of God's Holy Spirit or the testimony of scripture.

C-19. The best analogy I can think of right now is being "politically correct." Modern Pharisees get all over people for not using the right pronouns, which is like not washing your hands according to what somebody has decided is the "right" way to do it. Well, I'm with Jesus. It's what's in the heart that counts.

C-20. No matter how helpful or meaningful religious traditions can be, they do sometimes get in the way of hearing the will of God. Those of us who are religious leaders, in particular, need to be like Jesus in discerning whether a given tradition is helping or hurting the church to be what God wants it to be.

C-21. It is our job as pastors to constantly review the tradition of our elders, whatever that may be, to bind it or to loose it, whichever is necessary, to tell people as Jesus did, "This is God's commandment, this is just a human precept."

C-22. Jesus tells "church leaders" that they don't have a clue what the real problems and needs of his disciples are. I've said the same thing to the bigwigs in our denomination.

C-23. Jesus says some pretty harsh things to his disciples sometimes, but he's not going to let the Pharisees attack them. Same here. I can rail against my sheep from the pulpit, but I'd lay down my life for them if the wolf came around.

C-24. Every Sunday I look out over my congregation and think, "Are they getting this, or are they just going through the motions?" Jesus seemed to have the same doubts about the religious people of his day. That's comforting, I guess.

C-25. I wish I had the courage to do what Jesus does—tell hypocrites to their face what God thinks of them. What does this mean to me? It convicts me for not being more like Christ.

C-26. Jesus models boldness in proclaiming the Word, drawing on scripture, and applying it to an existential situation. He's not trying to win any popularity contest.

C-27. How can we get people to quit worrying about what is wrong with everybody else and just look to God with thanksgiving and praise?

C-28. I tell people religion is not about getting cleaned up on Sunday morning for God. It's about getting our hands (and clothes) dirty out in the world, doing what God calls us to do.

C-29. We need to preach the Word, even if people would rather just hear homey stories and take part in religious rituals. What they need may not be what they want. They need to hear us preach the Word of God.

C-30. Our church has a tradition of potluck suppers and rummage sales that I think are more important to some than the law and the gospel combined. In seminary I thought I would be a prophet but now I feel like a guest speaker at a religious club. So I have to ask, if Jesus were the pastor here—what would he have to say?

C-31. I've felt like Jesus does here when outsiders disparage members of my church. They may have their problems, but they're my responsibility and if anyone's going to disparage them I want it to be me.

C-32. We need to distinguish between what is essential (the gospel) and what is nonessential (*adiaphora*).

C-33. People tend to prize what is familiar above what is necessary. Jesus challenges us to sacrifice tradition and follow God's will.

C-34. Some of our traditions are good, some are bad, but none are as important as the Word of God.

C-35. Jesus offers grace, to comfort those whom hypocrites assail with their legalism.

C-36. Jesus' last sentence here is explained in terms of what follows—condemnation of Corban. He doesn't mean to say that tradition always voids commandments.

C-37. Some things are worth fighting about and others aren't. We should not trouble the faithful over meaningless details (like liturgical preferences or speaking in tongues). These things just divide the church. But God's commandments are eternal and people who are faithful to Jesus do not try to compromise them.

C-38. What would Jesus do? He would denounce shallow worship, false doctrines, and compromised ethics. So should we.

C-39. Jesus says that we are not called to live according to the tradition of the elders but according to the Word of God.

C-40. Pastoral ministry walks the fine line between affirming ritual and transcending it. We must be alert to the creeping presence of hypocrisy, when what should be matters of the heart become meaningless. Jesus affirms ritual that expresses the heart, denounces that which does not.

C-41. I find that people are always tempted to put tradition ahead of scripture. Tradition can be important, but we must find ways of evaluating the traditions of *our* elders to see if they are what God still wants us to do today. Scripture is timeless.

C-42. I always try to distinguish in my preaching between "Thus says the Lord" and "Thus says your pastor." I hope my words are good, but they are not God's.

C-43. We might ask, What is it that defiles our hands today? Is it failure to keep all the p's and q's that certain religious authorities think are so important, or is it failure to do justice and love mercy—the real commandments of God? Jesus tells us what our priorities should be.

C-44. Jesus shows me the need to distinguish between what is of man and what is of God.

C-45. I don't think you can say what the story means without looking at Isaiah to see what it says. Prophecy is being fulfilled in the obstinacy of Israel and their rejection of the Messiah.

C-46. The story presents Jews as petty and legalistic. This is not true.

C-47. The story suggests that Christians are superior to Jews because they don't keep kosher laws. Personally, I find that offensive.

C-48. I don't know why you chose this text. It is one of many anti-Semitic passages in the Bible. The representation of Pharisees is historically inaccurate. They were not given to hypocrisy or casuistry. And, certainly, they did not *abandon* God's commandments in favor of human traditions.

C-49. The issue of whether Christians should keep the Jewish law was a big one in early Christianity. Mark is writing for Gentiles, and so, of course, he wants to make the point that the law is no longer valid, except certain moral precepts like the Ten Commandments. Of course, this is contradicted elsewhere in the Bible and it's probably not what Jesus would have thought either. One hopes that in the next millennium we will get behind this kind of squabbling over who is most faithful to God and that Christians and Jews will benefit from each other's strengths. They have a lot to teach us, especially about tradition and law—the very things this text rejects.

C-50. What do I think it means? Christians are good. Jews are bad. They don't really worship God. He won't hear their prayers, and they're all hypocrites. That's what it means. Do I believe it? No, I do not.

## LAY RESPONSES

*Mark 7:1-8 Eating with Defiled Hands*

L-1. I can identify with Jesus' disciples. They don't seem to know what all the right religious traditions are, or maybe they just don't care. Jesus says it's what's in their hearts that counts.

L-2. I was on our Altar Guild and the pastor fussed at me for not putting things in the right place on the right day. My God, why does it matter?

L-3. In Jesus' day the leaders of the church were the hypocrites and that is sometimes still true. Do they really worship with their hearts or is it just a bunch of head knowledge? I don't always know what to do, but I'm pretty sure I'm a disciple and not a Pharisee.

L-4. I try to follow Jesus, but like his disciples, I don't keep all the rules. Sometimes I don't know them and sometimes I just don't do them. This story offers hope to people like me.

L-5. If the church tried to tell me how to wash my hands, I wouldn't do it either.

L-6. We still hear two voices, one that accuses us and one that gives us grace. Will we listen to Jesus or the Pharisees?

L-7. We have one decision to make: follow Jesus or the Pharisees. The Pharisees offer us rules and Jesus offers us life.

L-8. It comforts me to know that I don't always have to get everything right to please Jesus.

L-9. This story encourages me and gives me hope. The disciples are not very religious in an outward way but they are not hypocrites either. I think I can say that about myself too.

L-10. It motivates me to re-examine my own choices regarding religious practice. Which are really important? The disciples forego empty rituals that don't count.

L-11. The story reassures me that Jesus accepts me because of who I am and not because of what I do (or don't do).

L-12. I must admit, it troubles me. Maybe the disciples don't need to keep the traditions of their elders, but maybe they'd be better off if they did. Those old traditions can have a lot of meaning if you take time to understand them. They didn't become traditions for nothing.

L-13. If I were one of Jesus' disciples, I would be pleased to hear him tell the Pharisees, "Back off, don't be so picky. Take the log out of your own eye first."

L-14. There are so many Pharisees in our world today. Every time I turn on the TV or the radio, I hear them trying to tell me how to live. Jesus says, "Enough already!"

L-15. It always amuses me to hear Jesus call religious leaders "hypocrites." They always think that we are hypocrites because we say we're Christians but don't keep all their rules. Well, now the shoe's on the other foot.

L-16. This happens to me, too. I get my hands dirty just living in this world. (I mean, with sin). I need to wash them but not like the Pharisees. I need to wash in the blood of the Lamb.

L-17. Being a disciple of Jesus means we keep his commandments not the commandments of men (or women).

L-18. I know exactly how the disciples felt. They got in trouble for doing what Jesus thought was important instead of what their bosses thought was important. I could tell you stories about the place where I work.

L-19. Jesus accepts disciples even when their hands are defiled. Praise God! That's me. A "disciple with hands defiled."

L-20. The world tells us, "You can't eat until you wash your hands." In other words, you have to make yourself clean first before God will accept you. But Jesus accepts us the way we are.

L-21. Pastors and other church leaders are always criticizing everyday Christians for one thing or another. I hear Jesus saying, "Leave them alone. They're doing the best they can."

L-22. I am a Christian who doesn't like the tradition of the elders. I don't want to do things just because the church did it this way in the past. That's the main reason people don't come anymore. Get with the times.

L-23. You can wash everything in your house and you still won't be clean if you don't know Jesus. The Pharisees washed the outside and not the inside. Disciples have Jesus in their hearts and are clean within.

L-24. I am always amazed at the pettiness of organized religion—what happens when the heart is gone and just the outer shell remains. Jesus' disciples worship him with their *hearts* and hands and voices.

L-25. I'm embarrassed to admit that I have a lot in common with the Pharisees. I worship with my lips but don't always mean it. I guess I'm a hypocrite too.

L-26. The story convicts me of my own sin, judging others without first judging myself.

L-27. Shame. Guilt. When my heart is far from God, I don't admit it but just keep pretending, worshiping "in vain." This one really nails me.

L-28. I'm confused. Are we *not* supposed to do anything in church that comes from "humans." What about the Bible itself? It's the Word of God but people wrote it.

L-29. I find it frustrating that Jesus would be so quick to condemn people who are honoring God "with their lips." I don't feel spiritual all the time; nobody does. I think what's important is that you go and worship whether you feel like it or not.

L-30. Jesus sounds like a Pentecostal here who thinks that it doesn't matter what you say or do if your heart is in it. This is annoying and I can't believe that it would be right if we had the whole story. Other places he tells people to keep traditions (every jot and tittle). If this was all we had, I wouldn't like him very much.

L-31. The story is discouraging to those of us who value ritual and liturgy. "Human" tradition can come from God and help God's people. It is way too easy to label "hypocrisy" things that you don't appreciate but that might be very meaningful to others.

L-32. Do we abandon God's commandments and hold to human traditions? Do I? This verse is disturbing, one I need to think about.

L-33. The Bible is more important than anything else. Everything else is just the thoughts of humans. We need to make sure we are keeping the Word. That's what Jesus is saying to us.

L-34. Jesus says we are hypocrites if we go to church and keep all the human traditions but don't do what God commands.

L-35. I was raised Catholic and so I know about "human traditions." I visited a Greek Orthodox church and that's even worse. I used to be one of these people that Jesus says to them, "You hypocrites! Why don't you just do what God says?"

L-36. I worry that I will become one of the Pharisees. Church doesn't mean what it used to mean to me. The hymns I loved and the people I knew are all gone. Everything looks different. I still go and I still worship God, but I mean it less and less.

L-37. This is the question I have been asking my pastor in this class he is teaching about what we believe. Most of the stuff about all the creeds and the sacraments and infant baptism isn't in the Bible. I don't say it's wrong, but Jesus says "in vain do they worship me teaching *human precepts* as doctrine." That's scary. Where is this passage, because I want to show it to him.

L-38. Well, I'm not the one to ask because I haven't done very good at pleasing God or humans either one. I'm probably the biggest hypocrite of all. If this grace stuff doesn't work then I am in big trouble.

L-39. I know I would be one of the Pharisees, not one of the disciples.

L-40. Hypocrisy is the cancer of Christianity. Here are two ways we get this sickness: (a) worshiping in style without substance; (b) teaching unbiblical doctrines. If we avoid these things, we might avoid becoming hypocrites (though there are other ways too).

L-41. It makes me pray, "Lord Jesus, let me honor you with my heart and let me keep your Word. And keep me from judging others."

L-42. The whole point seems to be that we should not judge other people like the Pharisees do. We've got enough to do worrying about ourselves.

L-43. I need more of Jesus not more religion.

L-44. What are our seminaries teaching? Preachers today don't know the Word but they know a lot of human ideas. They can tell you what this theologian said. I want to know what God thinks.

L-45. Love is what's important, not all these customs. Did the Pharisees act very lovingly? I don't think so. There are better ways to criticize people. Anyway, Jesus loves his disciples and they love him.

L-46. Well, I'm glad I'm not Jewish because I wouldn't want to have to worry about all those things. I don't know if they still do that today, but it's so much better to just be able to trust in Jesus and know that I am saved.

L-47. Praise the Lord! Before I got saved I tried to please God in lots of ways too, but now he lives in my heart and I know that he is my Lord and Savior. The disciples must be already saved here (they have answered his call) because they seem to know what the Pharisees don't, that washing cups won't get you to heaven.

L-48. First, it reminds me that it is by grace alone that I am saved. Second, it gives me a heart of compassion for God's own people (the Jews) who are still trying to please him with their religion of rules instead of just believing in the Messiah whom he sent to them.

L-49. It angers me to see how Jewish people are described. I know Jewish people who keep these rules—washing pots and things like that. I don't think they are hypocrites. It's just their way of worshiping God.

L-50. Why are the Pharisees always the bad guys? Don't Christians have enough hypocrites of their own?

## Analysis of Responses

I don't know what you might have noticed in your survey of this data. Many people pick up on the last five responses offered by the clergy (C-46–C-50), all of which discern a potential for anti-Semitic rhetoric at work in the text. The same may be said of the last two lay responses. Other interesting themes surface as well, but I am going to suggest now that we focus on one particular facet of these responses: empathy choice.

Let us look together at the first few instances of Clergy Responses:

*C-1. The folks in my church always say, "We've never done it that way before." Jesus wants me to tell them, "Human traditions are less important than God's commandments."*

This person seems to be saying, "I ought to be like Jesus and tell the people in my church what he tells the Pharisees in this text."

*C-2. Scripture is more important than human traditions. People don't want to hear that, but it's true (and it's my job to tell them).*

This person seems to be saying, "My job is to be like Jesus and tell people what he tells the Pharisees in this text."

*C-3. I need to be a prophet of mercy, not judgment. People hear enough condemnation already. Jesus affirms those who the world calls "unclean."*

This person seems to be saying, "I need to be like Jesus, a prophet of mercy to those who are called unclean rather than a voice of judgment like the Pharisees in this text."

*C-4. Jesus attacks the hypocrisy of religious legalism and expects us to do so as well.*

This person seems to be saying, "We ought to be like Jesus by attacking the hypocrisy of religious legalism as he did."

We could keep going, but the point becomes fairly obvious. The clergyperson in C-5 seems to be saying, "I need to be like Jesus by doing three things that he did." The clergyperson in C-6 seems to be saying, "My job is to be like Jesus and protect my church from evil forces the way he defended his disciples against the Pharisees." All of these clergypersons were asked, "What does this story mean to you?" and their responses indicate that they found meaning in the story by way of *empathy with Jesus.* In the examples we just reviewed, such empathy appears to have been idealistic: the respondents assumed that in some way, shape, or form, they *ought* to be like Jesus and they explored what the story might mean when considered from that perspective. In a few other examples, the empathy actually seems to be realistic: C-9 can "easily relate to what Jesus faces here." But, in any case, the story was experienced in light of some perceived or possible connection between the respondent and the character of Jesus.

You can put this to the test and read through the responses again to see if I am right in my analysis. I admit that there is some guesswork involved, but I think that empathy with Jesus is discernible for the first forty responses (C-1–C-40). In many cases, the connection is actually made explicitly; in others, I think that it is clearly implied. For instance, C-32 thinks the meaning of the story is that "we need to distinguish between what is essential (the gospel) and what is nonessential (*adiaphora*)," but that is almost certainly what he or she thinks Jesus does in this story—so, again, the point seems to be "we need to be like Jesus." It is more difficult to discern what empathy choice might lie behind the final ten responses, but I *think* that C-41–C-44 are hearing the words of Jesus from the perspective of the scribes and Pharisees—and then stating their intention to distance themselves from the latter. If that is the case, these readers are actually empathizing with the scribes and Pharisees, albeit somewhat reluctantly or with appropriate humiliation. As for the last six responses (C-45–C-50), I would say that these persons are reacting to points of view that they attribute to the author of the story rather than to any of the characters within the story. Thus they are engaging the story in a completely different way: they refuse to enter the world of the story and identify with any of its characters because they have identified it as a world they do not care to inhabit. They exemplify what some literary critics call "resistant reading," a subject to which I will return briefly later (page 66).

For now, let us just note that even a cautious analysis of the Clergy Responses allows us to identify Jesus as the empathy choice for about four-fifths of the clergy who took part in this study. These results become more striking when we compare them with the responses of the laity.

Again, let's look at the first few instances of lay responses:

*L-1. I can identify with Jesus' disciples. They don't seem to know what all the right religious traditions are, or maybe they just don't care. Jesus says it's what's in their hearts that counts.*

This person seems to be saying, "I am like the disciples in this story, and so I find what Jesus says with reference to them to be meaningful."

*L-2. I was on our Altar Guild and the pastor fussed at me for not putting things in the right place on the right day. My God, why does it matter?*

This person seems to be saying, "I am like the disciples in this story in that I have had an experience analogous to what they face here, and so I think that what Jesus says in their defense applies to me."

*L-3. In Jesus' day the leaders of the church were the hypocrites and that is sometimes still true. Do they really worship with their hearts or is it just a bunch of head knowledge? I don't always know what to do, but I'm pretty sure I'm a disciple and not a Pharisee.*

This person seems to be saying, "I'm fairly confident that I am like the disciples in this story, in contrast to many church leaders who are like the Pharisees."

*L-4. I try to follow Jesus, but like his disciples I don't keep all the rules. Sometimes I don't know them and sometimes I just don't do them. This story offers hope to people like me.*

This person seems to be saying, "I am like the disciples in this story, and so the hope that I see offered to them is offered to me as well."

You get the point. These responses all assume empathy with the disciples of Jesus rather than with Jesus. In most cases, such empathy is realistic rather than idealistic. Instead of reading the story from a perspective that assumes, "I ought to be like Jesus," these laypersons appear to have read it from a perspective that assumes, "I actually am like the disciples." Why would this be? Don't laity think they ought to be like Jesus?

Let's leave that question aside for a moment and look at something else. My analysis suggests that only the first twenty-four responses (L-1–L-24) were derived through some degree of empathy with the disciples of Jesus. The next responses (L-25–L-42) seem to assume an identification with the scribes and Pharisees that is even more explicit than what I detected for a handful of clergy responses above (C-41–C-44). Let's look at a few of these together:

*L-25. I'm embarrassed to admit that I have a lot in common with the Pharisees. I worship with my lips but don't always mean it. I guess I'm a hypocrite too.*

This person seems to be saying, "I am like the Pharisees in this story, so Jesus' condemnation of them applies to me too."

*L-26. The story convicts me of my own sin, judging others without first judging myself.*

This person seems to be saying, "I am convicted of sin because I realize that I am like the Pharisees in this story."

*L-27. Shame. Guilt. When my heart is far from God, I don't admit it but just keep pretending, worshiping "in vain." This one really nails me.*

This person seems to be saying, "I experience guilt and shame because I realize that what Jesus says to the Pharisees in this story applies to me as well."

In a few cases, the connection might be less obvious. For instance, in L-28–L31, the respondents do not explicitly say "I realize that I am sometimes like these Pharisees" but they do appear to be engaging the words that Jesus speaks to the Pharisees in the text as though those words were addressed to them.

I offer no judgment regarding empathy choice for the last eight lay responses (L-43–L-50). These respondents may be interacting with various themes in the narrative, but I am unable to determine with any certainty that they have identified more closely with one character than with another.

Our results, then, may be summarized as follows:

| Empathy Choice: | Clergy | Laity |
| --- | --- | --- |
| Jesus | 40 | 0 |
| Disciples | 0 | 24 |
| Pharisees | 4 | 18 |
| Other | 6 | 8 |

What shall we make of all this? The zeroes in the table are particularly striking. Is it not remarkable that almost half of the laity would read this story from the perspective of Jesus' disciples, but *none* of the clergy would do so? Or that four-fifths of the clergy would identify with Jesus in this text, while *no* layperson would do so? For that matter, why would laity, who are not leaders of religious institutions, be four times more likely to empathize *realistically* with the Pharisees than clergy who (like the Pharisees) *are* leaders of religious institutions? Indeed, is it not a tad ironic that while only four clergypersons saw themselves as identifiable with the religious leaders in this story, six laypersons specifically identified clergy they knew as identifiable with those characters (L-2, L-3, L-15, L-21, L-37, L-44; see also L-5, L-6, L-7, and L-14)?

## Surveying the Gap (Empathy Choice)

We must be careful not to make sweeping observations on the basis of a single study (with a relatively small sample).

There is, of course, a degree of artificiality imposed by the process, which does not take various contextual factors into account. I did not, for instance, ask the clergy, "What does this story mean to you *as you think about preaching?*" Nor did I ask the laity, "What does this story mean to you *when you hear it read in worship?*" I grant that asking the questions in those ways might yield different results. My hope was to uncover some fundamental (albeit adjustable) tendencies. So, with those acknowledged caveats, let me summarize a few points that I think are worthy of further consideration.

First, let us note that clergy do seem to be more likely than laity to empathize with the character of Jesus when they read or hear Gospel stories. I have found this to be true with other texts besides this one, though the distinction is not usually as dramatic as it was in this instance. I have heard all sorts of explanations for this, ranging from psychological (clergy have messianic complexes), to pragmatic (clergy have vocations that involve doing the kinds of things that Jesus does in the Bible), to spiritual (clergy are more Christlike). I am in no position to adjudicate between such conjectures, and I have no causal theory of my own to suggest. I merely note that, with obvious exceptions, it does seem to be the case. Clergy may benefit from learning this about themselves (particularly since empathy choices are usually made subconsciously), and they may also benefit from recognizing that it is less likely to be true of their parishioners. It may seem natural to clergy to read Gospel stories from a perspective that asks, "How am I like Jesus?" and "How should I be more like Jesus?" Indeed, it may seem almost self-evident to clergy that this is the right or best way to read such stories. But the majority of laity do not automatically employ that sort of reading strategy; they do not find it natural to do so, and they certainly do not seem to regard such a stance as the right or best way to create meaning for themselves out of the data that the text provides. Personally, I attach no value judgment to such tendencies. It is not necessarily a good thing or a bad thing that clergy are often inclined to empathize with Jesus when they read Gospel stories, and it is neither a good thing nor a bad thing that laity are less inclined to do so. But you might want to be aware of the general tendency and check to see if holds true for you. If it does—or if it doesn't!—you may learn something about yourself.

A second and possibly related point is that we may note a greater propensity toward *realistic* empathy on the part of laity than clergy in this study. The clergy seem more inclined toward *idealistic* empathy, which, of course, could be one reason they were more likely to identify with the character of Jesus. Is this because clergy are more idealistic in their general outlook on life? Are laity more realistic? I doubt that we need to go that far. My studies on empathy have revealed that realistic empathy trumps idealistic choices when the basis for the realistic connection is obvious or strong. Even people who would be naturally inclined to identify with the hero of a story may be drawn to identify with the victim or the villain if there are striking points of contact. Thus, if they ever make a film about James Bond or Spider-Man or Sydney Bristow rescuing some nerdy Bible professor, I suppose I might find it difficult to maintain my usual penchant for imagining myself in the guise of rescuer—I will just have too much in common with the rescuee. While this is generally true for all readers, however, it seems to be *especially* true for laity— at least, when we are considering responses to biblical stories. The point for homiletics may be simply this: if laity are offered a number of empathy choices, they tend not to take the idealistic route when a realistic one presents itself.

With this in mind, let us look again at the character roles the story in Mark 7:1-8 offers its readers as empathy choices. The *religious leaders* (scribes and Pharisees) are portrayed as petty and judgmental legalists and are denounced as hypocrites. The *disciples* of Jesus are portrayed as lax with regard to what is presented as a minor matter of religious observance, and they are criticized by religious leaders for this. *Jesus* is portrayed as coming to the defense of his disciples by quoting scripture and perceptively discerning the difference between God's expectations and what are merely matters of human tradition. Given these options, a majority of clergy chose to empathize idealistically with Jesus: the meaning of the story for them was connected to a sense or assumption that they should be like him. I am now suggesting that one reason the laity did not follow suit in this instance may be that the other characters in the story offered realistic connections that were sufficiently strong to override idealistic impulses. The question then becomes, Why were these connections stronger for the laity than for the clergy?

With regard to the religious leaders, I suspect that most clergy have addressed the problems of hypocrisy and judgmental legalism more intentionally than laity have. They view hypocrisy and judgmental legalism as major vices that would undermine their very vocation. As such, I think that most clergy have either steeled themselves against these offenses or, at least, they have convinced themselves that they have done so. Clergy may be intensely aware of their inadequacies, but very few clergy consider themselves to be hypocrites or petty legalists. Laity appear to be more likely to own up to those failings.

With regard to the disciples, I suspect that "being criticized by religious authorities" is a more common experience for laity than for clergy. This is not because clergy do not get criticized—they do, but my sense is that the complaints come more often from below than from above: clergy may hear from dissatisfied parishioners on a regular basis, but they often function on a day-to-day basis with a relative lack of oversight from whatever ecclesial authorities their particular denomination places over them. In any case, this study suggests that many laity can relate to the experience of being criticized by religious leaders for infractions that they consider to be minor or meaningless.

About half of the laity who participated in this study found this to be an experience they thought they shared with the characters in the Gospel story. None of the clergy read the story from the perspective of people who felt that they had been unduly criticized by religious authorities.

Finally, I think the most important thing to take away from this study is a solid realization that empathy cannot be assumed, predicted, or controlled. Preachers need to realize that the people in the pews may be hearing the story from a different perspective than they do. What this means for you is that a sermon that seeks to build on what you take to be a self-evident connection with the text is likely to fail—the assumed connection may not be self-evident for many parishioners. To complicate matters further, we may note that even those who made the same empathy choice responded to the story in diverse ways. For example, laity who identified with the Pharisees in Mark 7:1-8 were variously embarrassed (L-26), shamed (L-27), convicted (L-26), confused (L-28), frustrated (L-29), alienated (L-30), discouraged (L-31), affirmed (L-35), worried (L-36), scared (L-36), or provoked to further thought (L-32). That would be quite a range of emotions for any one sermon to address—and we are not even considering the various responses of all the laity who empathized with the disciples! The bottom line, of course, is that no sermon can effectively address so many far-flung concerns. Some homiletical triage is necessary—choices must be made. So: polyvalence is a reality, and it can be a problem. Now, let's see if there are ways in which it might also work *for* us.

### Empathy Choices: Some Points To Remember

- clergy are generally more likely to empathize with Jesus in Gospel stories
- laity are more likely to empathize with the disciples or other characters

- clergy are generally more inclined toward idealistic empathy choices
- laity are more inclined to make realistic connections with characters they identify as similar to themselves

- clergy appear less likely to empathize with characters who exhibit the faults of hypocrisy or judgmental legalism
- laity are more likely to own up to those faults in themselves—and are also more likely to attribute them to modern-day clergy

- clergy appear less likely to identify with characters who are criticized by religious authorities
- laity readily identify with characters who are criticized by religious authorities apparently regarding this as a common, shared experience

## Bridging the Gap (Empathy Choice)

I offer three specific suggestions.

**Cast the scriptures**. Begin sermon preparation by employing a reading strategy I call *casting the scriptures*. I mean *casting* in the sense of dramatic production: casting a play. First read the biblical story, ask yourself what the story means, and then consciously identify the character with whom you have empathized. If this story were being performed on the stage of your life (so to speak), this is the character you would most naturally seek to play: this is the role with which you tend to identify. Why? Is the empathy realistic or idealistic? If you think about things like this regularly when engaging scripture texts you might learn some interesting things about yourself.

But now—and this may be the more important part— read the story again, trying out for a different role. Cast the story differently in your mind and force yourself to empathize with a different character and to experience the story from that character's point of view. Inevitably, this leads to new perceptions, ones that you may have missed but that might be readily available and meaningful to your parishioners. The point is simply to expand horizons and notice potential for meaning. Casting the scriptures helps us to discern polyvalence, to identify a fuller range of options by which audiences can and do create meaning for themselves out of the raw materials the text provides. Sometimes, at least, you might choose to go a completely different route with your sermon than you would have discerned through your default empathy identifications.

**Be explicit, if necessary.** Once you have discerned a range of possible empathy choices that engage meaning at different levels, there are two ways that you might want to go. You might determine that for this particular sermon one avenue of identification works better than any other. In that case, if the effectiveness of your sermon *depends* upon a particular empathy choice, be explicit in promoting this. Most people can switch gears when prompted to do so. Thus, you might just ask in your sermon, "How do you think so-and-so felt when this happened?" Or, better, you might take the congregation through the story one more time, specifically relating it from the particular character's point of view. It would be possible, with the Mark 7:1-8 text, to retell the story from the perspective of the scribes and Pharisees, focusing on *why* this purity matter was an issue to them and perhaps relating modern-day anecdotes that would be roughly analogous (e.g., a person whose family always prays before meals visits the home of some supposedly devout person—maybe a pastor—and notices that his or her family does *not* pray before the meal). By retelling the story in this way, you humanize these characters and help parishioners to find points of contact with them: parishioners who couldn't care less about ritual hand-washings may nevertheless be able to imagine themselves thinking and acting like the scribes and Pharisees in other analogous situations. Then, of course, the rhetorical trap has been laid for Jesus' words regarding hypocrisy and/or the prioritizing of human traditions over God's commandments. *If* this is the route you have chosen to go—*if* you want to preach a sermon convicting people of hypocrisy and judgmental legalism—then you should recognize that the effectiveness of such a sermon depends upon getting your audience to empathize realistically with the scribes and Pharisees. You need to be explicit and intentional about establishing that particular empathetic connection.

Of course, it would be possible to craft a very different sermon that depended on establishing realistic empathy with the disciples in this story—and you could do that in a similar fashion, retelling the story from their perspective and relating it to modern experiences with which parishioners could likely relate. My studies suggest that many laity would make such a connection easily and naturally—indeed, about half would have made it already without your help. If, however, you wish to preach a sermon that depends upon idealistic empathy with Jesus, you should definitely be explicit about encouraging that connection: "Let's take a look at what Jesus says and does in this story and ask what we would need to do to be more like him . . ." This is not difficult. Almost all parishioners will be able to make such a connection when prompted. All I'm saying is, they may need to be prompted.

**Allow for multiple responses.** I indicated there are two ways to go with a sermon after identifying the diverse possibilities for empathy identification. One is to be explicit about promoting the identification necessary for the particular route you have chosen to take. The other is to preach a sermon that recognizes the potential for diverse connections and allows hearers to make meaning for themselves accordingly. I took this approach when I was recently asked to preach on John 6:1-13 for the opening convocation of what my denomination calls a Global Mission Event. A diverse group of people had gathered for several days of worship, workshops, and other presentations organized around a central theme of world mission. There were large numbers of youth and adults, as well as an eclectic mix of laypersons, pastors, and missionaries. The purpose of my sermon was to provide some initial orientation to what we might all get out of the next few days together. I decided to preach a sermon in three parts, telling or retelling the story of Jesus feeding the five thousand three times. Each time I focused on a different character in the story and tried to draw specific connections to persons in my audience: (1) The hungry multitude in the story might represent those who come to an event such as this one asking, "For what do I hunger?" and "Who will feed me?" (2) The disciples of Jesus represent those who ask, "What do I have to offer?" and "Is it enough?" and (3) The little boy with the basket represents those who are brought to ask, "What am I willing to give up?" This was not a "three-point sermon" in the traditional sense, for I did not assume that all three points would be applicable to everyone. I would have been delighted if everyone had found *one* of the suggested avenues to be meaningful, and I was willing to trust the Holy Spirit to aid each listener in discovering what God's Word to him or her might be.

Empathy is a primary mode for readers to connect the meaning of biblical stories with meaning in their own lives. Preachers who understand empathy may draw upon likely connections to tease out the contemporary significance of certain elements within the biblical text. To the extent that empathy is unpredictable and uncontrollable, it can be the undoing of a well-intended sermon. Still, the diversity of empathy choices holds more promise than peril for preachers who are aware of the reality. By exploring different empathetic possibilities, we can uncover avenues to meaning that we might have neglected. Then we may choose either to promote one particular perspective on the text or to throw the story open to a panoply of persuasions. Either way, we provide our listeners with tools to mine meaning for themselves from the raw material of the biblical text.

# Chapter Four

# Message or Effect: The Meaning of *Meaning*

What do we mean when we speak of *meaning*? One major reason that texts or stories mean different things to different people is that people differ in what they regard as constituting *meaning*.

I discovered this almost accidentally while conducting experiments similar to the one discussed in the last chapter. I would ask people "What does this story mean to you?" and as I tried to sort out the wildly disparate responses I received, it sometimes occurred to me that some people had not answered the question at all. For example, in the clergy responses to Mark 7:1-8, one respondent (C-48) wrote, "I don't know why you chose this text. It is one of many anti-Semitic passages in the Bible. The representation of Pharisees is historically inaccurate. They were not given to hypocrisy or casuistry. And, certainly, they did not *abandon* God's commandments in favor of human traditions." My initial reaction to such a response was dismissive. Regardless of whether the complaints about the text (and my selection of it) might be valid, the person did not answer the question. Instead of telling me what the text *means*, he or she complained about its historical inaccuracy. At best, I thought, this person is telling me what the text *doesn't* mean or *shouldn't* mean.

On further reflection I realized that all of the respondents were in fact answering the question—quite literally, they were reading the biblical story, reading my question about it, and providing me with what they considered to be an answer to that question. But my question itself was a text and *all* texts are subject to polyvalent interpretation. Some people took the question "What does this story mean to you?" differently than others. Some people told me how they felt about the story. Some told me why they didn't like the story. But these were all responses to the question of meaning. Literary critics maintain that distancing oneself from a text is as much an act of interpretation as embracing it; they address this phenomenon under the heading "resistant reading," according to which a reader more or less intentionally chooses to defy the rhetoric of a narrative and creates a meaning for the story by responding to it in ways contrary to what the author apparently intended. They may do so because they object ideologically to what they perceive to be an underlying message or moral of the story or because they object aesthetically to the manner in which a story is apparently intended to affect them. A preacher who is insensitive to gender issues might encounter resistant reading from a parishioner who perceives the underlying message of the sermon to be an endorsement of patriarchy. A preacher with a penchant for sentimentality might encounter resistant reading from a parishioner who finds a maudlin anecdote to be amusing for its "camp" quality.

We are not primarily interested in resistant responses, but their mere existence does serve to illustrate the plurality and unpredictability of interpretation. Furthermore, what has just been said about different types of resistant readings applies to more traditional avenues for reception as well.

Literary critics sometimes speak of "compliant reading" as the opposite of resistant reading—and this is what most of us probably practice most of the time. Unless prompted to do otherwise, we seek to receive narratives (or sermons) in the manner that appears to be expected of us. Nevertheless, we may have very different conceptions of just what "the manner that appears to be expected of us" entails.

This could get deep—but it won't. Hermeneutics and epistemology are philosophical subdisciplines within which many brilliant persons—Jacques Derrida, Michael Foucault, Walter Ong, Paul Ricoeur—have explored the nature of *meaning* and how meaning is communicated. I draw somewhat simplistically upon them now to make only one distinction that will be relevant for our immediate purposes. Here are two different conceptions of meaning:

a. *meaning as message.* The meaning of a text may be described in essentially *cognitive* terms. Understanding the meaning of the text entails identification of the *point* that is made therein.

b. *meaning as effect.* The meaning of a text may be described in essentially *affective* terms. Understanding the meaning of the text involves recognition of its *impact* on those who receive it.

Do you remember what Bill Clinton said in his deposition before the federal grand jury, when he was accused of lying about sex in a manner that ultimately led to his impeachment? His most quotable quote was, "It depends on what the meaning of *is* is." Well, now you can be as articulate as President Clinton. When someone asks you what something means you can respond, "That depends on what *means* means."

## Message and Effect

Examples of "meaning as message" can be found in most biblical commentaries. There, the goal of interpretation is usually to disclose the message of the text. This, furthermore, seems to be a cross-cultural phenomenon. In previous chapters, I have given some examples of how people in different countries interpret the parables of the Prodigal Son (pages 15-27) or the Good Samaritan (pages 35-38). We observed some differences with regard to what Americans or Russians or Tanzanians thought the main points of these stories were—and we witnessed some disparity with regard to which points might be considered major and which minor—but everyone seemed to agree that the goal of interpretation should be to figure out what those points were. In every culture, the meaning of each of these stories was pretty much equated with a message (or messages) that the story under investigation was supposed to convey.

Linguist Roman Jakobson suggests that the core of every communication act consists of three components:

| Sender | ← | Message | ← | Receiver. |
|---|---|---|---|---|
| With written literature, this triad becomes | | | | |
| Author | ← | Text | ← | Reader. |

Thus, when we speak of meaning as message, we are envisioning the text as a vehicle for conveying a message from author to reader. The meaning of the text is essentially defined by its *author*. Readers who get the message that the author intended to convey are said to understand the text. Readers who do not get that message—who discern a different message than the author meant to convey—are said to misunderstand the text. The author decided what the text is supposed to mean and the reader's job is to figure this out.

But now let us consider some instances of the other type of meaning, what we have called "meaning as effect." Examples of this concept of meaning can be found in many popular movie reviews. Critics often try to predict how audiences will react to a film: Will they laugh or groan or weep? Will they be inspired or bored? The reason that film critics do this is because they generally serve the interests of moviegoers and they recognize that most moviegoers are more concerned with how a film will affect them than they are with what point or points it may seek to convey. Some films, of course, are more message-laden than others but even when that is the case, receiving the message is but part of a total experience. In 2004, millions of movie-goers said that they found the movie *The Passion of the Christ* to be meaningful; others clearly did not. Those who did find the movie meaningful no doubt appreciated the messages it conveyed, but there was often much more to their reaction than that. The movie's fans and supporters talked about how watching the movie made them *feel* ("beloved of God," "unworthy of grace," and so on). Likewise, the movie's detractors sometimes objected to the messages they thought were being conveyed, but their complaints often went deeper. For example, some described the film's gruesome and gory depiction of violence as an assault on the senses that they experienced as vile or exploitative. In either case, *The Passion of the Christ* was one of the most message-heavy movies to hit theaters in a long time and yet the *meaning* of the movie could never have been summarized in a list of propositions or "message statements." The *meaning* of the film, both for those who liked it and for those who did not, tended to be defined in terms of its impact or effect on particular audiences or audience members.

The predictions that movie critics offer in film reviews tend to be contextual, based on an assumed audience appropriate to any given film's genre; critics don't usually try to predict how fans of "horny teenager movies" will react to highbrow period pieces (or vice-versa). Thus, a "meaning as effect" model seeks to understand what Roman Jakobson would call an "act of communication," from the opposite end of the **Author ← Text ← Reader** paradigm than that which we assumed for a "meaning as message" model earlier. The meaning of a work is now viewed from the perspective of its audience or recipients. Indeed, meaning is defined by recipients. If I tell my wife, "That was a funny movie," I do not mean, "The people responsible for making this movie intended for it to be humorous" (though they probably did). I mean, "I experienced this movie as humorous." That this is the case may be ascertained from the fact that I might in some other instance say, "That movie wasn't funny," even when I am well aware that the producers intended their film to be a comedy. When I say, "It wasn't funny," I mean "It wasn't funny *to me*."

Well, you are probably wondering what any of this has to do with homiletics—or even with the different ways in which clergy and laity understand the Bible. We will get to the latter point directly, and to the former eventually. Even now, however, you might just pause to ask yourself, Are sermons more like Bible commentaries or popular movies? Is the *meaning* of a sermon to be found in the message that it conveys—or in the effect that it has on its audience? And is the meaning of a sermon ultimately defined by its sender (the preacher) or by its recipients (the congregation)?

## Words and Pictures

I think that there is a general tendency in our culture to associate *message* with words. I find that if I ask students about the meaning of some essay or article, they almost always respond by telling me what the central point or thesis of the piece is. That is probably what you would do too. But if I were to ask you about the meaning of Gustav Mahler's *Fourth Symphony* or Jackson Pollock's *Lavender Mist*, how would you respond? Most people, I think, find those works of art to be meaningful not because they serve to communicate particular messages but because they affect recipients in aesthetic or even emotional ways. Indeed, persons who *don't* find such works meaningful sometimes don't seem to be able to connect with them on precisely those terms. I heard someone complain that classical music is boring. "I always daydream when I go to the symphony," she said. "It's because there are no words, nothing to keep my attention." Well, personally, I *like* daydreaming and while it is true that most classical symphonies do not have as recognizable a plotline as a typical Andrew Lloyd Webber musical, I find that they can inspire and focus my daydreams in a manner that I would term meaningful. Or, just spend a day at the Museum of Modern Art sometime and see how many people shake their heads at some abstract or nonrepresentational masterpiece, muttering "I just don't get it" or (*very* revealing) "What's the point?" The equation of message-less with meaning-less is a symptom of our times: we have been so conditioned by a wordy society to define meaning as message that it is difficult to shift gears, even in our off-hours at the museum or the theater.

Stories are usually told with words, but the words serve to create images or pictures in our minds. Stories often convey messages, but they are also valued for their aesthetic, emotional, or even transformational effects. Stories are hermeneutical hybrids: they may have morals, but their meaning cannot be expressed through simple summaries of those morals.

Rudolf Bultmann is rightly regarded as one of the greatest New Testament scholars of the twentieth century. I have learned much from him, but I never did get his desire to "demythologize" all of the miracle stories in the Bible by explicating their meaning in terms of existentialist propositions that the tales embodied or illustrated. Before encountering Bultmann (in college), I had wrestled with the writings of Marshall McLuhan in high school. McLuhan taught that "the medium *is* the message," and I am convinced that this is true—one cannot take the message of a miracle story and express it as a philosophical dictum without radically altering its meaning. The medium through which the message is expressed is intrinsic to its meaning.

I caricature Bultmann's program with the following analogy: imagine that some high school English teacher were to notice that many of today's teenagers do not appreciate or understand Elizabethan poetry. The poems, this teacher insists, are very meaningful, but their archaic literary style has become an obstacle to reception for contemporary audiences. Many high school students consider imposed rhyme schemes or metrical patterns to be artificial and stilted forms of expression. So, let us replace Shakespeare's sonnets with short paragraphs summarizing the poignant and often lovely points that the Bard was attempting to make. I hope you will agree with me that such an enterprise would be preposterous. There is more to a poem than the point of the poem: *how* it says what it says is as least as important as *what* it says.

To be fair to Bultmann, he did not want to *replace* the miracle stories with his existentialist interpretations of them. Still, the meaning of a story cannot be divorced from the medium through which it is told: miracle stories are expected to inspire awe in a manner seldom attributed to summaries of existentialist philosophy. That is part of the meaning of a miracle story—it shocks and frightens; it inspires awe.

This is true of all stories—even parables, which (along with fables) are prime examples of stories that convey messages. Look at the example on the next page.

Luke (or Jesus) tells us what the message of the story is. So, if the message were all that was important, why bother telling the story at all? Why not just report that Jesus said, "You should pray always and not lose heart." We might say that the purpose of the story is to *illustrate* the message and render it memorable. Yes, but is that all?

Try having a Bible study on this passage some time and I can guarantee you many things will come up that have little to do with "praying always and not losing heart." Why is God portrayed as an unrighteous judge?

| Story | Message |
|-------|---------|
| "In a certain city there was a judge who neither feared God nor had respect for people. In that city there was a widow who kept coming to him and saying, 'Grant me justice against my opponent.' For a while he refused; but later he said to himself, 'Though I have no fear of God and no respect for anyone, yet because this widow keeps bothering me, I will grant her justice, so that she may not wear me out by continually coming.'" (Luke 18:2-5) | The need to "pray always and not to lose heart." (Luke 18:1) |

Are we supposed to imagine that God is reluctant to help us? Or does Jesus simply realize that it sometimes seems that way? Is he, perhaps, being ironic—poking fun at the way we mortals construe divine restraint? But why would Jesus choose to depict us (petitioners) as "a poor widow"? Is it because we are helpless before God? Is he urging humility? Or does he mean to critique our assumptions regarding the marginalized? The mere fact that the story evokes such questions, without answering them, indicates that it is more than just an illustration of the message, "Pray always and do not lose heart." The capacity of the story to evoke questions like these is part of its meaning.

Compare this Parable of the Widow with another story in Luke's Gospel that conveys essentially the same message:

| Story One | Story Two |
|---|---|
| "Suppose one of you has a friend, and you go to him at midnight and say to him, 'Friend, lend me three loaves of bread; for a friend of mine has arrived, and I have nothing to set before him.' And he answers from within, 'Do not bother me; the door has already been locked, and my children are with me in bed; I cannot get up and give you anything.' I tell you, even though he will not get up and give him anything because he is his friend, at least because of his persistence he will get up and give him whatever he needs." (Luke 11:5-8) | "In a certain city there was a judge who neither feared God nor had respect for people. In that city there was a widow who kept coming to him and saying, 'Grant me justice against my opponent.' For a while he refused; but later he said to himself, 'Though I have no fear of God and no respect for anyone, yet because this widow keeps bothering me, I will grant her justice, so that she may not wear me out by continually coming.'" (Luke 18:2-5) |

The basic message of these stories is the same, but we might question whether the stories *mean the same thing*. Consider the differences: Story One features second-person narration and Story Two, third-person narration; Story One employs a paradigm that involves dialogue between social equals while Story Two employs one that involves dialogue between nonequals; Story One presents a supplicant whose concern is for others (feeding a visitor), addressing a potential provider whose counter-concern is also for others (waking children) while in Story Two both the supplicant and the provider exhibit concern for themselves. Given these differences, do the stories have the same meaning? People who equate meaning with message might assert that they do—the same meaning (message) is simply packaged differently for pedagogical reasons (e.g., to reach different audiences). But people who equate meaning with effect would probably not view the matter that way: they would view the so-called packaging as intrinsic to the essential meaning of the stories. The stories may convey the same message, but not with the same effect.

Elsewhere in Luke's Gospel, we hear that the repentance of a sinner is like what happens when a man with a hundred sheep abandons ninety-nine to find the one that is lost (15:3-7). And then we hear that it is like what happens when a woman with ten coins frantically sweeps her house to find the one that has become lost (Luke 15:8-10). Again, the message that the author intended to convey might be the same for each of the two stories, but why did Luke bother to tell two stories that make essentially the same point? At the very least, we can affirm that he wanted the second story to reinforce the message of the first through pedagogical redundancy, and affirming just this much implies a recognition that the second story is intended to have a different effect (i.e., reinforcement) on its readers than the first. And we can probably go further: if we consider the differences between the stories (man/woman, sheep/coins, etc.), we will likely discover other ways in which the stories could have diverse effects on different readers, in spite of conveying identical messages. My point is just this: the fact that Luke includes such "doublets" in his Gospel implies that he was operating with a concept of meaning inclusive of effect as well as message.

## Luke 3:3-17: Preaching of John the Baptist

Now we are ready to consider another experiment that I conducted concerning the different ways that clergy and laity hear or respond to the Bible. This one concerns a story found in Luke 3:3-17, an account of the preaching of John the Baptist. The experiment proceeded along the same lines as that discussed in chapter 3 earlier. I gave fifty clergy a sheet of paper on which the text of Luke 3:3-17 (New Revised Standard Version) was printed, along with the question: "What does this story mean?" A sample of the sheet is found below. I gave an identical sheet to fifty laypersons. Once again, I sought diversity in both the clergy and lay samples and yet maintained equivalent ratios regarding the more obvious factors of social location (age, race, gender, etc.) such that the two groups of people were remarkably similar except that one group consisted of fifty clergy persons and the other of fifty laypersons.

This experiment did differ from the one involving Mark 7:1-8 in one significant way. When I prepared the handout for use in the study, I decided to delete the words *to you* from the question at the top of the page. Instead of asking "What does this story mean to you?" I asked simply, "What does this story mean?" As it turns out, the most interesting revelation of the study came as a result of this minor change in wording.

All one hundred answers to the question, "What does this story mean?" are printed on the pages that follow. Once again, you may want to browse these before continuing with my analysis of the comments. There are many interesting points, but I actually think that what I found to be most striking will be fairly obvious to almost any observer.

## Luke 3:3-17: What Does This Story Mean?

[John the Baptist] went into all the region around the Jordan, proclaiming a baptism of repentance for the forgiveness of sins, as it is written in the book of the words of the prophet Isaiah, "The voice of one crying out in the wilderness: 'Prepare the way of the Lord, make his paths straight. Every valley shall be filled, and every mountain and hill shall be made low, and the crooked shall be made straight, and the rough ways made smooth; and all flesh shall see the salvation of God.'"

John said to the crowds that came out to be baptized by him, "You brood of vipers! Who warned you to flee from the wrath to come? Bear fruits worthy of repentance. Do not begin to say to yourselves, 'We have Abraham as our ancestor'; for I tell you, God is able from these stones to raise up children to Abraham. Even now the ax is lying at the root of the trees; every tree therefore that does not bear good fruit is cut down and thrown into the fire."

And the crowds asked him, "What then should we do?" In reply he said to them, "Whoever has two coats must share with anyone who has none; and whoever has food must do likewise." Even tax collectors came to be baptized, and they asked him, "Teacher, what should we do?" He said to them, "Collect no more than the amount prescribed for you." Soldiers also asked him, "And we, what should we do?" He said to them, "Do not extort money from anyone by threats or false accusation, and be satisfied with your wages."

As the people were filled with expectation, and all were questioning in their hearts concerning John, whether he might be the Messiah. John answered all of them by saying, "I baptize you with water; but one who is more powerful than I is coming; I am not worthy to untie the thong of his sandals. He will baptize you with the Holy Spirit and fire. His winnowing fork is in his hand, to clear his threshing floor and to gather the wheat into his granary; but the chaff he will burn with unquenchable fire."

## CLERGY RESPONSES

*Luke 3:3-17 Preaching of John the Baptist*

CC-1. Luke reports something that happened in the first century. Before Jesus began his ministry, John the Baptist called people to repentance. He attracted quite a bit of attention, drawing large crowds out in the wilderness, where he practiced a ritual baptism. The movement apparently took on messianic overtones, though Luke reports that John denied any identification of himself as the messiah, speaking only of one who was still to come.

CC-2. John fulfilled the prophecies of the Old Testament regarding a forerunner, just as Jesus would fulfill the prophecies of a coming Messiah.

CC-3. The main point comes in the last paragraph. John may have been a prophet, but a greater one was coming.

CC-4. The point seems to be that knowledge of God's salvation caused people to take account of themselves. Even John's baptism brought this response, "What shall we do?" How much more would the coming of Jesus bring people to ask this question.

CC-5. The emphasis is clearly on judgment. John promised that there would be a judgment and that Jesus would carry it out. Those who don't bear fruit get thrown into the fire.

CC-6. It means that God will have a people prepared, even if he has to make them from scratch. God is willing to start over and make children from stones if need be. He sent John to preach judgment and Jesus to clear the threshing floor. He stopped at nothing to get people ready.

CC-7. Why was it necessary for John to come first? Just to fulfill the scriptures? No, he had to put people's hearts right with God so they would be receptive to Jesus.

CC-8. Luke tells us that God sent John to prepare people for the coming of Christ. He did this by demanding fruit worthy of repentance. He also announced that Christ was about to arrive.

CC-9. Luke says that John came into a world filled with expectation because they were looking for their Messiah, but later when the Messiah came they did not recognize him and even John did not recognize him.

CC-10. The picture we get is one of people who are spiritually hungry. They would do whatever it takes to please God, but they were so worked up that they confuse the messenger with the message. John is pointing them to Jesus, not to himself.

CC-11. Luke describes the scene that stood as the threshold for the coming of Jesus. People were looking for salvation but they still had to be prompted to act on it and to repent. So God sent John to help get them ready.

CC-12. When John came he fulfilled the prophets and preached God's Word faithfully—but he was really just the last of the Old Testament prophets himself. He himself said that Jesus would offer something new, something more powerful. The new covenant is one of spirit and fire.

CC-13. Perhaps the most obvious (and therefore overlooked) point here is that *baptism* is mentioned for the first time. Until now, the mark of belonging to God's people was circumcision, which automatically left out half of the human race. John deserves credit for being the one to see how foolish this was and to replace circumcision with baptism, a symbol of salvation for *all* flesh, male and female. Jesus may have been influenced by this.

CC-14. John understood Jesus to be the powerful new agent of God, but he was wrong about what Jesus would do. Jesus did not come to throw the chaff in the fire, but to become a friend of sinners and to welcome them. John expected a Judge, not a Savior.

CC-15. John thinks religion is a matter of keeping the right rules. Won't he be surprised when Jesus does come and refuses to keep all those rules himself?

CC-16. John spoke of transformation—valleys being filled, rough ways made smooth, etc. He said this is what would happen when God came into the people's lives. There would be a moral transformation of who they were. Jesus is the one who would effect this through the baptism in the Holy Spirit.

CC-17. It talks about a "wrath to come" but also says that "all flesh" will see God's salvation. Luke is a universalist who uses metaphors of judgment existentially. The wrath is experienced now, but eventually all will be saved.

CC-18. All of the things that John says to do have to do with money—sharing possessions and not taking from others. This sets up Luke's pronouncement that Jesus came to bring good news for the poor.

CC-19. Luke wrote his Gospel to defend Christians against Roman persecution. He presents John as a prophet who encourages good citizenship (take care of yourselves, obey the laws, don't cause trouble).

CC-20. Luke is "preparing the way" himself for the transfer of salvation from Jews to Gentiles, which he will narrate in Acts. Being a descendant of Abraham no longer counts, but receiving the coming Messiah.

CC-21. Luke shapes his account of John the Baptist's ministry to make clear that John is subordinate to Jesus. John's role is clearly that of a forerunner. His ministry is similar to that of Jesus, but only preparatory. John himself identifies Jesus as the more powerful one whose sandals he is unworthy to untie. Most likely, Luke is trying to forestall or combat subordinationist Christology that may have regarded Jesus as a disciple of John the Baptist since, after all, Jesus was baptized by John (a historical fact Luke neglects to report!).

CC-22. Luke does not say that the *people* need to prepare the way for God to come to them. Rather, God sends John to prepare the way. This is an act of sheer grace. God says, I am going to come to my people and nothing will keep me from them. My servants (John, Jesus?) will do everything necessary for me to come to them.

CC-23. Luke seems to like the question: "What then should we do?" The people ask it here, and if I am remembering right, they ask it again on the day of Pentecost (which may be referred to here also—in the reference to baptism with the Holy Spirit). I think it comes up other places, too, but I would have to check. Luke really wants us to ask that question, in response to whatever it is that God has done.

CC-24. Luke knows the Parousia has been delayed, and he writes to people who may be troubled by this. Here he wants to emphasize that the judgment of God *will* come eventually, even it seems to have been delayed. This judgment will establish justice in all the earth.

CC-25. The way Luke tells the story of John the Baptist, he can offer people salvation if they repent and live right, but Jesus will come and offer salvation by a cross.

CC-26. We read about John in all the Gospels, but only Luke shows him to be concerned with details, sharing your coat, etc. (the third paragraph). So he wants us to get down to the nitty gritty and ask, What difference does this really make?

CC-27. Luke's intent seems to be brought out in the phrase "*all* flesh shall see the salvation of God." In this story there are Jews and Romans and "even" tax collectors all coming to baptism and all being promised the Holy Spirit.

CC-28. Luke wants to say that salvation is (potentially) for all. God has no favorites and there are no "chosen people." But everyone alike must bear the fruit of repentance.

CC-29. Why does Luke try to connect the work of John the Baptist to the prophecy in Second Isaiah? I would need my library to study this, but it seems that he sees John as fulfilling the Isaianic vision of universal salvation. And, of course, he does this by speaking of judgment and wrath because judgment *brings* salvation.

CC-30. Luke takes the traditions of John the Baptist and uses these as a link between the eras. On the one hand, John fulfills the Old Testament prophecies; on the other, he himself prophesies of Jesus. In John, Luke shows us what he regards as the best of the old and the promise of the new. It is interesting that baptism becomes the symbol that unites these.

CC-31. The story is found in the first part of Luke's third chapter. It must be considered in light of chapters 1 and 2, where Luke presents the announcements and births of John and Jesus in ways that beg comparison. John is great but Jesus is greater. The same contrast is now made here with regard to their ministry. Luke's agenda is to promote Jesus over John with a view to first-century rivalries between disciples of the two leaders.

CC-32. Luke is interested in explaining repentance so that everyone could understand what it meant. There are no confusing ethical dilemmas here. Luke just told his church that God wants people to help the needy, be honest at business, and refrain from violence. People could either do these things or not do them. The church today could benefit from emulating this simple and direct approach.

CC-33. It is curious that Luke indicates that John's baptism brings forgiveness of sins. I think he also said this earlier when John was born. If John brings forgiveness, why do we need Jesus? In Luke, Jesus seems to serve some other role, not bringing forgiveness but the kingdom of God. He brings liberation to captives and enacts social justice.

CC-34. Luke calls for action, with a sense of immediacy ("even now"). He wants people to believe that what they do has consequences both in the present and forever.

CC-35. Luke says that Jesus will baptize people in the Holy Spirit and then later shows how this is fulfilled (in the book of Acts). So, from the very start, he's saying that Christians should be Pentecostals.

CC-36. Luke makes clear that neither John nor Abraham is the one the people need. Jesus is the mightier one who gives the spirit. Later, in Acts, people baptized by John have to get rebaptized in the name of Jesus in order to have the Holy Spirit.

CC-37. Luke is trying to tell us that the grace of God is not cheap. It calls for a response, that is for repentance and amendment of life.

CC-38. Luke wants us to tell people that God expects something from them. Faith ought to impact life and make a difference in how we live.

CC-39. The "way of the Lord" is a way of salvation, but that way needs to be prepared. Those who know Christ need to prepare the hearts of others so that the Lord Jesus can come to them.

CC-40. I think the message of the text for my church would concern the proper way to prepare for the coming of the Lord today—and I don't mean the apocalyptic second coming, but how does our society prepare to welcome Christ? If we knew he was coming to our home or town or congregation, what would we want to fix up before he got here?

CC-41. This text always comes up in Advent, a week or two before Christmas when no one wants to hear about judgment or repentance or "the wrath to come." I think it's misplaced, so I always preach on the Old Testament (messianic prophecies).

CC-42. I remember preaching on this one Christmas season and I asked, What do we do to get ready for Christmas? (buying presents, sending cards, baking cookies). Then I asked, What if we were as concerned about being ready for Christ (preparing the way) as we are for Christmas?

CC-43. Amid all the harsh words are kernels of grace: all flesh will see salvation; God can raise up children from stones; the wheat will be gathered into the granary. I think we have to look for the gospel in a text like this one and not be swayed by all the fire and brimstone that may have worked better in another time and place.

CC-44. I think of that song: There ain't no mountain too high or valley too low to keep God away from us.

CC-45. The lesson is that God wants a people prepared. Perhaps this is why Jesus has waited so long to return. Can we hasten that day by living like God's people should?

CC-46. The message for people today is that the baptism Jesus offers is one of spirit *and* fire. He empowers us to live for him but also burns up everything that keeps us from doing that.

CC-47. The most striking part of the story to me is the sort of "anti-evangelism" in the second paragraph. Today, churches are so concerned about getting members or making converts that they lower standards to attract the masses. But John turns away people who ask to be baptized—until they bear fruit worthy of repentance.

CC-48. I think the message for today is that we need to preach law as well as gospel. We need to be bold as John and lay out the requirements of God. This is what "prepares the way" for people to hear the word of salvation through Christ Jesus.

CC-49. There are many verses but I am drawn to this one: "not worthy to untie the thong of his sandal." John was the one prophesied long ago and people had been waiting for him for hundreds of years. He was the greatest man ever born of woman but even he was not worthy to untie the sandal of our Lord.

CC-50. To be honest, John sounds like some kind of TV evangelist, all law and no gospel. This text really can't be read on its own. It's part of a bigger story because John is only the forerunner to Jesus. I think I would tell people, "You see, if not for Jesus, this is what we would get." This is the Bible without Christ (which come to think of it is what we usually get from TV evangelists).

## LAY RESPONSES

*Luke 3:3-17 Preaching of John the Baptist*

LL-1. John was trying to tell people that Jesus was coming just like many preachers today are trying to get us ready for his return, but people don't listen any more now than they did back then.

LL-2. I am confused why, if the whole purpose of baptism is forgiveness of sins, people have to repent first and stop sinning. If you can do that, you don't need forgiveness of sins. Maybe this is the difference between Jesus and John the Baptist. Jesus offers forgiveness to people who are lost in their sins and really need it.

LL-3. John is talking to Jews who thought that they could be saved just by being born that way. I actually heard a Christian preacher say this once, too, that all the Jews got some kind of free ticket for salvation just because they're Jewish. Well, this verse definitely disagrees with that. The only way to the Father is through the Lord Jesus Christ.

LL-4. When I read this story I am inspired by the portrait of what a biblical preacher really can be. John the Baptist proclaims the word in a way that deals with the everyday stuff of people's lives—how to serve God wherever you are, be it as a tax-collector or as a soldier. It's a ministry of law and gospel. He talks about forgiveness and salvation but also about repentance and judgment. And most important, he points away from himself, directing people to Jesus. This is the type of witness I would like to be.

LL-5. We need to warn people to get ready for the coming of the Lord. If we don't, who will?

LL-6. It encourages me to be more forthright about sticking up for what I believe. John did this and people respected him for it.

LL-7. I am humbled by John's example because he was the greatest man ever born and yet he says he is unworthy to untie the Lord's sandal. If he is unworthy, how much more are we? But we still think we are so important sometimes. It is all about the Lord and not about us.

LL-8. I agree with John when he says, "you must bear *fruit* worthy of repentance." Too many people think that just being baptized or coming to church is enough, when there is no fruit of the Lord's presence in their lives.

LL-9. I have felt like a voice crying in the wilderness before— like I was the only one who cared about what was *right* (not just what would *work* or make money). You do just want to think of everyone else as a brood of vipers, but we have to leave the judgment to God. Actually, it says that here too.

LL-10. This story upsets me because the crowd that comes to be baptized gets lambasted, which is just like what happens when we go to church and the preacher tells us how bad we are. I want to say, "Hey, at least we're here. That should count for something." But then what he says about not depending on your ancestors really hits home, because I think sometimes we just think we can be baptized as babies and then ride to heaven on our parent's faith. Now he says we have to bear fruit worthy of repentance. So the crowd asks, "What then should we do?" which is exactly the question I'm asking now.

LL-11. It shocks us into asking if we are ready for our Lord to come.

LL-12. We have a choice of getting baptized with spirit or with fire and how we live our lives now determines which it will be.

LL-13. It scares me, obviously, because even though we are told all the time that we are saved by grace, here the Bible says it depends on how you live.

LL-14. It is very "in your face." It's like, the Lord is coming, and if you're not ready, you're really going to be sorry. It doesn't worry me, though, because I think that kind of religion is just exploitative.

LL-15. I actually find it very comforting, which may seem surprising, but with all the talk of judgment, the first paragraph says, "all flesh will be saved," so I don't think we have to be afraid.

LL-16. It warns us of the need to prepare a way for the Lord in our own individual lives. It's not enough that God chose Abraham and others in the Bible but now he wants to come into our hearts and we have to make room for him there.

LL-17. Not all of it applies to me, but the part about "whoever has two coats" does because I probably have five or six coats. I'm not a literalist, but it seems that almost everyone in America has more than they need of many things while people in other countries don't have enough. For us, "preparing the way of the Lord" probably means finding more equitable ways of distributing the earth's resources.

LL-18. It moves me to get serious about acting on faith. The time may be short. We know what is expected of us. Now, we just have to do it.

LL-19. I gotta say it provokes me, in more ways than one. It makes me think, what do I have to do to get ready for the Lord? And, it irks me somewhat because just when I thought I was ready, something else comes up, and the Holy Ghost says, You aren't ready yet. So I get provoked a lot by this story and by other texts that tell me what I need to do.

LL-20. You probably showed us this text to try to scare us into getting more serious. It is scary when I read it and think about whether or not I am ready to meet my Maker, but to be honest with you I don't think about it that often and neither does anyone else I know. There are just too many other things to do in a day that there is no time to think about things like this.

LL-21. It simply challenges us to always be ready for the Lord to come, whenever that may be. Of course, there is no way we ever get it down perfect, but there is always room for self-examination and improvement.

LL-22. I think that if we are always worried about whether we are "prepared" for the Lord or not, we will miss the bigger picture. None of us is ever worthy of Christ, not even John the Baptist himself. So being prepared means just opening our hearts to him to receive his forgiveness.

LL-23. What are the valleys, what are the mountains, what are the hills in my life that keep God away from me? What crooked things do I need to make straight, what rough ways need to become smooth for me to see his salvation?

LL-24. The story challenges us to put our words into action and live the way God wants us to live: helping the poor, being honest in our jobs, and not trying to push others around. This is all pretty simple, but how many people even do this much?

LL-25. I always look for promises in the Bible and here I find two—salvation and the baptism in the Holy Spirit. Many people in our world have not experienced either. Many people in churches have only the first. Why settle for just "avoiding hell" when Jesus offers so much more?

LL-26. The story shakes me out of my comfortable little world where everything seems okay as long as I don't ask too many questions. It forces the ultimate questions of judgment day upon me already, ahead of time, and asks for consideration of how I will fare in that balance. Even spiritualized as symbol or metaphor, such imagery commands a response.

LL-27. It gives me pause to consider something I don't plan to think about until I'm a lot older, unless I land in the hospital with some terminal disease. Am I ready? Well, I'm better than some, worse than others. I don't know, but if I don't make it, wherever I go will be awfully crowded.

LL-28. He sounds like "a Baptist," if you'll pardon the pun, in that all he talks about is condemnation. I'm not afraid of God and no preacher will ever make me be. God is love. He doesn't throw people into fires to suffer forever and ever. Stories like this just make me sick. I'm sorry it's in the Bible, but there are a lot of things in the Bible that don't reveal the God of love.

LL-29. "Filled with expectation"—so am I. Not for John but for Jesus. Having been baptized, the way of the Lord is prepared for me, by faith, and I am ready for him to come, for me or for the whole world, anytime. I am ready.

LL-30. Our parents' faith does not save us. They can be saints, it doesn't matter. Everyone needs to be born again— PKs, everyone. We need to find the Lord ourselves, and he needs to make a difference in our lives—the fruit worthy of repentance.

LL-31. The ax and the winnowing fork are pretty scary. They terrify our conscience and I can only respond like Luther: "I am baptized."

LL-32. Like these people, I keep looking for something that I can do to earn my salvation. The gospel tells us that Jesus has done it all.

LL-33. I find it intimidating. Anytime we are asked, "Are you ready for the Lord to come?" the answer will obviously have to be no. I mean, who would claim that they are? That would be pretty arrogant. So, of course, we get intimidated and then dig in and try harder. We probably need to hear this now and then, but too much overkill and people just tune out. I think most people are doing the best they can and encouragement works better than threats.

LL-34. What strikes me is the juxtaposition between social responsibility and messianic enthusiasm. The people are all worked up over someone who is going to come and deliver them from all their troubles—but John tells them to focus on the present and help each other right now. If we take care of the present, the future will take care of itself.

LL-35. Well, if I'd been there, I would have been one of the "brood of vipers," I guess, so I suppose the meaning is that I better clean up my act and fast before the wrath of God descends. But this was a long time ago, right? Hasn't happened yet.

LL-36. It just angers me. Stories like this perpetuate the image so many people have of Christianity, that it is a judgmental religion, all about rules and punishment. Forgiveness gets mentioned once here and then is quickly forgotten.

LL-37. It fills me with excitement. We live on the brink of the future—our Lord is coming, with threat and promise. We wait for his arrival with fear and joy.

LL-38. It tells me that when all is said and done, there will be justice at last. I find this reassuring; it is the hope that lets us go on in a world where we do not see that justice now.

LL-39. It gives me hope for the future. I don't have much hope for the present. We're not doing a very good job of "preparing." But the Lord will come either way, whether we're ready or not.

LL-40. We cannot save ourselves but God can save us. If God can make children out of stones, then he can make us into whatever he wants us to be. He can baptize us in the Holy Spirit and purify us in the fire, sanctify us in his image till we are "done."

LL-41. I think the Holy Spirit must have picked this one because I have to admit it convicted me where it says the tax collectors shouldn't take more than they are owed, because that probably means that we ought to give them everything that they are owed.

LL-42. The ultimate question is, Are we chaff or are we wheat? There is going to be a day of reckoning, when everything is exposed.

LL-43. I find it a little threatening, like some of the stories in the Old Testament, but I think this was before Jesus died for us, and that changes everything. We are not going to get burned up just because we failed to do the things that these people get told to do. God is more merciful than that.

LL-44. I don't know what it all means, and I especially don't understand that one verse—"all flesh shall see the salvation of God"—because I thought that "flesh and blood cannot inherit the kingdom of God." It is not our flesh that gets saved but our soul. Our bodies just rot or get eaten by worms. Our soul goes to heaven and inherits the kingdom. So I don't have any idea what it means.

LL-45. I find it so amusing that the people want to follow John rather than Jesus. They still do that now, when they act like their pastor or some other leader is the messiah. They confuse the messenger with the one who really is the Message.

LL-46. I saw a button that said, "Jesus is coming—and is he *pissed!*" That about sums it up.

LL-47. I was baptized as a baby in a Catholic church and only later found out that the Bible says you must be baptized for repentance. People are not ready for the Lord if they have not repented and asked Jesus to come into their hearts as their personal Lord and Savior. Also, like it says here, they are not ready if they are still living in sin.

LL-48. It's hard to take such a story seriously in our world today because only crackpots believe this way: The end is coming soon! Prepare to meet thy doom! There must be a message somewhere for us, perhaps in the third paragraph with its counsel of wise and ethical behavior. I think we can all live that way whether we believe the end is coming soon or not.

LL-49. Stories like this make me mad. This is the kind of religion I was brought up with and there are too many bad memories associated with that kind of preaching. It's why I didn't go to church for years. If I went to church now and heard this one I would just walk out.

LL-50. "People get ready," Rod Stewart sang. I hope he heeds it. It would be nice to have him in the choir in heaven.

## Analysis of Responses

What do we make of all this? Here is an initial observation:

> Twenty-six of the clergy responses refer to Luke (the author of the story). None of the lay responses do so.

Why would this be? Is there something about the process of seminary education or the vocation of clergy that sensitizes people to identifying the titular author of a narrative? Is such sensitivity peculiar to biblical literature? What if I were to use one of Aesop's fables in a similar study? Would half of the clergy mention *Aesop* in their response? Would none of the laity do so?

Another observation:

> All fifty of the laypersons make some reference to *themselves* in their response: they employ a personal pronoun (I, we, me, us) in answering the question "What does this story mean?" Only twenty of the clergy do this.

Why would this be? Is there something about seminary education or clergy vocation that desensitizes people to personal reference? Again, would this phenomenon be peculiar to biblical interpretation? Or would it apply to other stories as well?

Before jumping to any conclusions on such matters, I decided to go back and check the data from my previous experiment, the one involving the story Eating With Hands Defiled (Mark 7:1-8). Were these statistical anomalies regarding a clergy preference for "references to the author" and a lay preference for "references to self (i.e., the respondent)" evident there as well. They were not. In that study:

> Only one of the clergy responses (C-49) refers to *Mark* (the author of the story). Again, none of the lay responses do so.

All but four of the clergy responses employ a self-reference in answering the question, as do all but two of the laity.

To visualize this data, look at the following table.

| | Mark 7:1-8 What does this story mean to you? | Luke 3:3-17 What does this story mean? |
|---|---|---|
| CLERGY: author-reference | 1 | 26 |
| LAITY: author-reference | 0 | 0 |
| CLERGY: self-reference | 46 | 20 |
| LAITY: self-reference | 48 | 50 |

Read the columns vertically. There was no significant difference in the responses of clergy and laity in the first experiment (Mark 7:1-8): compare 1 to 0 and 46 to 48. But there was, I think, a significant difference in those responses in the second experiment (Luke 3:3-17): compare 26 to 0 and 20 to 50.

I do not think the divergent results can be accounted for by anything intrinsic to the stories. I suspect, rather, that the different results are attributable to the different questions that were asked. The two words *to you* made a significant difference for clergy in determining how they responded to the story: When I asked "What does this story mean *to you*?" clergy showed a high propensity for self-reference and low propensity for author reference (46 "self" to 1 "author"). But when I asked simply "What does this story mean?" the propensity for self-reference decreased (from 46 to 20) and the propensity for author reference increased (from 1 to 26). This makes sense. The question "What does this story mean *to you*?" invites self-reference. We should not be surprised that wording the question this way increases the propensity for clergy to respond with self-reference.

Nevertheless, the wording of the question seemed to affect *only* the clergy responses. Laity showed a very high propensity for self-reference (from 48 to 50) no matter how the question was worded, and they showed *no* propensity for author-reference in either case. Inclusion or omission of the words *to you* had no discernible effect on how laity answered the question. How do we explain that?

My tentative conclusion is that laity demonstrate a tendency to read stories as applicable to themselves with or without prompting. Clergy, by contrast, demonstrate an ability to read stories as applicable to themselves when prompted to do so, but they often do not read them this way when they are not prompted to do so. The clergy *default*, if you will, is to read stories from the perspective of the author: when asked, "What does this story mean?" the clergy tended to tell me what they thought it meant to the author. Laity did not do this—indeed, not a single one did this. The laity simply assumed that when I asked, "What does this story mean?" I meant, "What does it mean *to you*?"

## Surveying the Gap (Message or Effect)

In this study, clergy seemed able to interpret stories either way—from the perspective of the author or from the perspective of the reader (themselves)—but their tendency was to go with the former unless the latter was specifically requested of them. Why would this be? Perhaps it has something to do with their training. Most seminaries have courses in exegetical method that focus on how *not* to read one's own situation or perspective into a biblical text. Seminarians are encouraged to avoid *eisegesis* (reading their own ideas *into* a text) and are taught to perform *exegesis* (reading the author's ideas *out of* a text).

Of course, as some recent seminary graduates will know, some of the newer exegetical methods do assume a *reader-oriented hermeneutic* rather than the traditional *author-oriented hermeneutic*: narrative criticism, reader-response criticism, and varieties of postmodern biblical criticism have been all the rage in the academy in recent years, and such methods have gained a hearing in some denominational schools. They tend to minimize or ignore concern for authorial intent in favor of questions regarding reception: How has the text been understood throughout history? How might it be understood by different audiences today? How would it be understood by an "ideal reader" or a "compliant reader" or a "resistant reader" (or any number of other imaginary readers that these methods posit for interpretive consideration)? If such reader-oriented methods continue to be taught in seminaries, the next generation of clergy may approach biblical texts differently than those who took part in the study reported in this chapter.

Regardless of whether that turns out to be the case, it strikes me as noteworthy that laity would evince the reader-oriented hermeneutic associated with some of these newer methods even though they have not been trained in those (or any other) scholarly approaches. They simply assume that the question of what a story means implies reflection on what it means to people who read it in the present day. Clergy, by contrast, tend to assume that the question of what a story means implies reflection on what it meant to its author. This is not to say that clergy are not interested in current meaning for contemporary audiences; obviously, they are. The point, I think, is that clergy prefer a two-stage process: first, identify what the author meant to communicate, and then extrapolate meaning for the present that is compatible with the author's intent. The laity, in this study, tended to skip the first step.

Both clergy and laity want the words of scripture to be relevant to contemporary situations, but clergy seek to identify such relevance through the discernment of contextual analogies, while laity do so through a relatively unmediated process of direct application. The clergy in this study often seem to have answered the question, "What does this story mean?" by identifying a message that the text would have conveyed within its original, historical context and then indicating how that message remains relevant for comparable situations in the world today. The laity display a greater tendency to engage the story as directly applicable to their lives apart from any consideration of whether the perceived points of contact are in keeping with what the author had in mind. In a great many cases, the laity in this study seem to regard the meaning of the story as identical with their reaction to it.

Let us acknowledge, again, the artificiality of the experiment. These laity were all participating in a controlled study. Had they been reading the Bible on their own or, say, preparing to teach a Sunday school class, they might have availed themselves of various aids that were not at hand and given consideration to matters that the parameters of this study prevented them from investigating. My point, in any case, is not to use this study as an occasion for demonstrating how laity need to learn basic principles for contextual interpretation of scripture. That could be a topic for another day. Right now, I would like to leave aside the question of whether clergy do this right or laity do it wrong. Let us simply note the difference. Perhaps it is only a question of "starting point": laity start with the reader when discerning the meaning of a text, while clergy start with the author. Perhaps. In any case, I believe that the distinction has implications important for preaching and ministry.

This whole matter becomes much more interesting when we realize that there is a close connection between the tendency toward reader- or author-oriented hermeneutics and the conceptions of meaning as effect or meaning as message that we discussed earlier (pages 67-75). The reader-oriented perspective tends to regard meaning as *effect*, while the author-oriented perspective tends to regard meaning as *message*. With that in mind, I encourage you to consider some of the language clergy and laity used to tell me what the story in Luke 3:3-17 means. I have taken key words from about half of the answers and placed them on the chart.

| The Preaching of John the Baptist (Luke 3:3-17): What Does This Story Mean? | |
| --- | --- |
| Clergy | Laity |
| Luke reports something (CC-1) | I am confused (LL-2) |
| The main point comes (CC-3) | I am inspired (LL-4) |
| The point seems to be (CC-4) | It encourages me (LL-6) |
| The emphasis is (CC-5) | I am humbled (LL-7) |
| Luke tells us that (CC-8) | I have felt like (LL-9) |
| Luke describes the scene (CC-11) | This story upsets me (LL-10) |
| The most obvious point is (CC-13) | It shocks us (LL-11) |
| It talks about (CC-17) | It scares me (LL-13) |
| Luke's pronouncement that (CC-18) | I find it very comforting (LL-15) |
| Luke wrote his Gospel to (CC-19) | It warns us (LL-16) |
| Luke shapes his account (CC-21) | It moves me to get serious (LL-18) |
| He wants to emphasize that (CC-24) | It provokes me (LL-19) |
| Luke's intent seems to be (CC-27) | It is scary (LL-20) |
| Luke wants to say that (CC-28) | It simply challenges us (LL-21) |
| Luke shows us what he regards (CC-30) | The story challenges us (LL-24) |
| Luke's agenda is to promote (CC-32) | The story shakes me (LL-26) |
| Luke indicates that (CC-33) | It gives me pause (LL-27) |
| He wants people to believe that (CC-34) | I find it intimidating (LL-33) |
| Luke says that (CC-35) | It just angers me (LL-36) |
| Luke makes clear that (CC-36) | It fills me with excitement (LL-37) |
| Luke is trying to tell us (CC-37) | It gives me hope (LL-39) |
| I think the message of the text (CC-40) | It convicted me (LL-41) |
| The lesson is that (CC-45) | I find it a little threatening (LL-43) |
| The message for people today (CC-46) | I find it so amusing (LL-45) |
| The message for today is (CC-48) | Stories like this make me mad (LL-50) |

The difference, I think, is compelling. Clergy answer the question "What does this story mean?" in cognitive terms that attempt to identify significant points or ideas that are being conveyed; for them, the meaning of the story is its *message*. The laity, however, are much more inclined to answer that question in affective terms that identify a reaction or response that they experience with regard to it; for them, the meaning of the story is its *effect*. Of course, this is not absolute, and the categories of "message" and "effect" are not mutually exclusive. Still, looking at these two lists side by side . . . the difference is remarkable.

Something similar can actually be detected in the responses to the story Eating with Defiled Hands (Mark 7:1-8) that we considered in our last chapter. In that study, I explicitly asked, "What does this story mean *to you*?" but even then very few clergy told me how the story *affected* them (I count only five who did: C-13, C-24, C-25, C-33, and C-47). I suspect this is because most of the clergy approached even this reader-oriented question from an author-oriented perspective and allowed that to mediate their response to the "to you" part of the question. This is only speculation. What is clearly demonstrable, however, is how several of the laity construed the question of meaning for that story (Mark 7:1-8):

This story offers hope (L-4)
It comforts me (L-8)
Encourages me and give me hope (L-9)
It motivates me to re-examine (L-10)
The story reassures me (L-11)
It troubles me (L-12)
It always amuses me (L-15)
I'm always amazed (L-24)
I'm embarrassed (L-25)
The story convicts me (L-26)
Shame. Guilt. (L-27)
I'm confused (L-28)

I find it frustrating (L-29)
This is annoying (L-30)
The story is discouraging (L-31)
This verse is disturbing (L-32)
I worry (L-36)
It makes me pray (L-41)
It gives me a heart of compassion (L-48)
It angers me (L-49)

### Message or Effect: Some Points to Remember

- clergy are more likely to consider meaning in terms of authorial intent
- laity are more likely to consider meaning in terms of reader response

- clergy are more likely to look for meaning related to historical, comprehensive, or typical situations
- laity are more likely to look for meaning related to contemporary, particular, or personal situations

- clergy are more likely to construe meaning as a message (what they learn from it)
- laity are more likely to construe meaning in terms of impact (how it affects them)

- clergy are more likely to identify relevance through contextual analogies
- laity are more likely to identify relevance through unmediated application

## Bridging the Gap (Message or Effect)

I now want to offer a few specific suggestions for how we might bridge this gap between pulpit and pew.

**1. Recognize and celebrate that laity want to be affected by scripture.** I think this study demonstrates that laity want the Bible to *do* something to them. They probably want the same from our sermons. They want something to happen—something more than just a transfer of information. This is consistent with a biblical understanding of "the Word of God." In the Bible itself, the Word of God is an active, dynamic force that never returns void but accomplishes that for which it is sent (Isa. 55:11). The Word of God does things: it cleanses, it heals, it creates, it judges, it saves. Thus, we should be pleased if our parishioners come to the Bible with a hope or even an expectation that it will do to them what the Word of God does: affirm them, rebuke them, comfort them, frighten them. That hope or expectation is consistent with the basic claim of all churches that the Bible is "the Word of God." Further, when laity say that they want their pastor to "preach the Word of God," I think that one thing they mean is, "I want his or her sermon to do to me what the Bible would do to me—I want it to do what the Word of God would do."

**2. Realize that message-oriented sermons fail to connect with the primary concerns of many laity.** People often appreciate messages—they find them interesting and provocative—but this study indicates that laity are less likely than clergy to identify the meaning of a story with the message that it conveys. It is possible, then, that a sermon articulating the essential message of a text will be less meaningful ("full of meaning") from their perspective than it is from ours. Let me try to illustrate the problem with the following scenario: imagine a congregation composed of the fifty laypersons surveyed for the study in this chapter. It is Sunday morning, and someone reads Luke 3:3-17 as the chosen text for the day. The responses collected on pages 84–89 provide us with a summary of what the members of the congregation are now thinking or feeling. Many of them are responding emotionally and aesthetically to the words that they have just heard: some have been comforted, some inspired, some confused, some frustrated, some angered. Now, an ordained minister steps into the pulpit, refers to the story just read, and proceeds (1) to tell everyone what *message* the author intended to convey to his original audience and (2) to identify (on the basis of this) a message that the story may now convey to us today. This may be done very well and the message disclosed may be an important one, but that does not change what is happening: the preacher is answering a question ("What is the message of the story?") that few people are asking. Meanwhile, the divergent effects that the story had on the listeners are gradually diluted as the sermon proceeds and perhaps forgotten by the time it reaches conclusion. At the end of the service, many will shake the minister's hand and say, "That was a good message." The parishioners will have received something—no doubt something worthwhile—but we are left to wonder whether something was lost in the process. Did the sermon do to these people what the Bible would do? Did it comfort, inspire, confuse, frustrate, or anger? Or was it simply interesting and informative?

**3. Be intentional about crafting sermons geared to produce specific effects.** Early in the preparation process, you might ask, "What effect do I want my sermon to have on people this week?" The chart on page 100 suggests a range of options—fifty-two suggestions or (if you like) one for every Sunday of the year. Hank Langknecht, professor of homiletics at my own institution, says that the *one* specific effect of every sermon should be "to gospel people." I like that, and I would regard my suggestions as fifty-two different ways of describing what that might mean: these are things that the gospel of Jesus Christ does. As to which of these or many other possible effects of the gospel one should aim for on any given Sunday, I would hope that such a decision would be made in dialogue with the text(s) for the day. The assumption is that you would do sufficient exegesis to determine what potential effects a responsible interpretation of the chosen text could be likely to generate. The pertinent post-exegetical question may be, "Which of the potential 'gospel effects' that this text might have on its readers do I want to see produced in my congregation?" That is a different post-exegetical question than, "Which of the messages that this author intended to convey to his original readers do I want to convey to my congregation?" By asking about *effect*, you force yourself to adopt the perspective of your audience and to think momentarily about the meaning of your sermon (and indeed of the text) in a way that is closer to how laity think about what is or is not meaningful. By contrast, if you begin the sermon preparation process by asking, "What message do I want my sermon to convey this week?" you will be coming at the enterprise from your own perspective and may develop a sermon that is more meaningful on your terms (i.e., that accords with your construct of what constitutes "meaning") than it is on theirs. The goal of a sermon may be . . .

| | | |
|---|---|---|
| to arouse confidence | to allay suspicion | to engender holiness |
| to provoke repentance | to repair relationships | to enact justice |
| to inspire generosity | to make peace | to manifest mercy |
| to evoke worship | to revive hope | to alleviate despair |
| to celebrate grace | to instigate loyalty | to purge corruption |
| to relieve disappointment | to motivate obedience | to mollify anguish |
| to invoke joy | to awaken love | to restrain sin |
| to encourage prayer | to comfort sorrow | to empower witness |
| to dispel gloom | to fortify commitment | to produce patience |
| to heal heartache | to strengthen devotion | to commemorate triumphs |
| to build community | to restore trust | to cultivate kindness |
| to generate enthusiasm | to calm fear | to prompt faithfulness |
| to assuage grief | to enable ministry | to stimulate compassion |
| to channel resources | to galvanize support | to facilitate fellowship |
| to kindle forgiveness | to create friendship | to spark anticipation |
| to instill humility | to spawn virtue | to renew pride |
| to sustain faith | to resolve conflict | to incite action |
| to foster gratitude | | |

**4. Allow the story to work for you.** One thing this study demonstrates is that biblical stories have the capacity on their own to produce a wide variety of effects. The laypeople who took part in this study did not hear sermons on The Preaching of John the Baptist—they simply read the biblical story and responded to it in remarkably diverse and often significant ways. The story itself generated those effects. If this is typical of biblical narrative (and I think it is), then to some extent your job may be to stay out of the way and allow the story to do what it can do better than you can. I have come increasingly to think of preaching as "the performance of scripture." I could almost define it as that. This does not mean that we simply memorize biblical stories and recite them (though that can be an effective way of "reading" the lesson). No, a sermon should expound the biblical story in a way that goes beyond rote repetition. But what does that mean? A reductionist approach to homiletics involves identifying a significant moral or point that the story serves to make and then delivering a talk on that topic (in accord with, perhaps, a three-point outline and appropriate illustrations). Instead of doing that, you might allow the structure of the story to determine the structure of your sermon. Preaching can take the form of retelling the biblical tale in a lively and dynamic way that accentuates certain points and explains others but preserves the inherent strengths of the narrative. Of course, this may work better with some texts than with others, but more texts actually have a narrative component to them than we are prone to recognize. Even epistle texts have a narrative infrastructure—there is a story that undergirds the letter writer's relationship to the congregation, and there is the grand meta-narrative of God's dealings with God's people. Preaching is storytelling—telling "the old, old story of Jesus and his love"—and stories are intrinsically transformational. If we want to preach sermons that will impact people's lives we should get in the habit of first looking for the story that is being told in any text and then looking for ways of retelling that story so that it can do a lot of the transformational work for us.

**5. Become familiar with exegetical methods that operate with a reader-oriented hermeneutic.** Most seminaries train their pastors in disciplines of historical criticism (e.g., source criticism, form criticism, and especially redaction criticism) all of which are oriented toward the goal of determining the authorial intention behind ancient texts. Such methods may be valuable and necessary for a proper interpretation of scripture, but even their most enthusiastic advocates often note a down side to their use in pastoral ministry. Their application involves a necessary distancing from appreciation for the relatively timeless effect or impact that stories can have on readers who receive them in contexts and under circumstances the author never imagined. This is true because these methods assume an author-oriented hermeneutic—they are designed to enable the interpreter to understand the text from the perspective of its author, which (for better or worse) is not the perspective from which many of our parishioners engage texts when they find meaning that affects or impacts their lives. Disciplines of literary criticism (e.g., narrative criticism, reader-response criticism, and postmodern criticism) tend to assume more of a reader-oriented hermeneutic that can get at what historical-critical methods fail to discern. This certainly does not mean that the literary methods are superior to the historical ones or that the reader-oriented hermeneutic is intrinsically preferable to an author-oriented perspective. The proper goal is to supplement what one already knows so as to have as complete a set of tools as possible. Personally, I find that historical methods merit primacy for purposes of theological interpretation but that literary methods are often more useful for preaching. Christian dogma should be expressive of the *message* of scripture and that message is best determined with exegetical methods derived from an author-oriented hermeneutic. But the performance of scripture that is often constitutive of preaching calls for knowledge of how stories work: how they achieve their intended effects and how analogous effects might be achieved in their retelling.

I think that the best "how-to" guides for achieving such an understanding of texts are:

Mark Allan Powell, *What Is Narrative Criticism?* Minneapolis: Fortress Press, 1990.

James L. Resseguie, *Narrative Criticism of the New Testament: An Introduction.* Grand Rapids: Baker Academic, 2005.

Sorry to recommend my own book, but I really do believe these are the two best works on the subject, especially for preachers who are interested in practical application. In addition, the single best book for illustrating how literary method applies to a particular Gospel is:

David M. Rhoads, Joanna Dewey, and Donald M. Michie. *Mark as Story: An Introduction to the Narrative of a Gospel,* 2nd ed. Minneapolis: Fortress Press, 1999.

A number of books are also available that explicitly address the connection between literary interpretations of scripture and preaching. These represent a range of theological perspectives:

Joel B. Green and Michael Pasquarello, eds. *Narrative Reading, Narrative Preaching: Reuniting Narrative Interpretation and Proclamation.* Grand Rapids: Baker Academic, 2003.

David L. Larsen, *Telling the Old, Old Story: The Art of Narrative Preaching.* Grand Rapids: Kregel Publications, 1995.

Richard W. Swanson, *Preaching the Gospel: Methods to Embody Biblical Storytelling Through Drama.* Cleveland: Pilgrim Press, 2004.

Richard F. Ward, *Speaking of the Holy: The Art of Communication in Preaching*. St. Louis: Chalice Press, 2001.

See also these two works on relating a sermon to the genre and intent (both message and effect) of the biblical passage:

Mike Graves, *The Sermon as Symphony: Preaching the Literary Forms of the New Testament*. Valley Forge: Judson Press, 1997.

Tom Long, *Preaching and the Literary Forms of the Bible*. Philadelphia: Fortress Press, 1989.

**6. Prioritize performance: delivery is as important as content.** If we think of a sermon as a vehicle for delivering a message—conveying to the congregation what we have decided is an important point made in the text—then content is clearly what is most important. In terms of delivery, the sermon need only be presented in a fashion that will be sufficiently clear and interesting for people to get the point: we need to keep their attention, and that's about it. But if we want to preach sermons that will affect people's lives, then the sermon becomes a *performance event*. For some years now, I have found myself slightly annoyed when I preach in our seminary chapel and the next day someone says, "I missed your sermon—can I get a copy of it?" I am flattered by the request, but I want to say, "No. You can't. I can show you the manuscript I used, but the sermon was an event that happened yesterday in chapel and if you weren't there, you missed it." If the only purpose of a sermon were to convey a message, then reading the manuscript would suffice. In fact, reading the manuscript might be a *better* way of getting the message, since one could reread it as necessary and with fewer distractions. But if a sermon is a performance event intended to affect people's lives, then what happens in that sermon can never be captured in a manuscript. We have much to learn from other performing artists in this regard: no singer would ever give people a sheet with lyrics to his or her songs and consider it a worthy substitute for having attended the concert: "Just read the words—you'll get what I was trying to say." We ought to think of ourselves as performing artists and prepare for preaching the way that singers and actors prepare for their public performances. An initial question to consider may be, "Do we spend as much time practicing a sermon as we do composing it?" Delivery is as important as content.

## Conclusion

As I travel about the country, I note that many churches do not even list a sermon in their bulletins anymore. Instead of a "Sermon" they have a "Message." I'm not sure what's up with that. I guess somebody has decided that the word *sermon* sounds too formal or stodgy and needs to be replaced with a contemporary synonym. I have no particular opinion about that. Words come and go and if the word *sermon* has truly served its time, I suppose we can retire it with dignity. But I am intrigued that people think *message* is the obvious synonym. I suspect that the pastors who hope to reach their congregations by replacing the word *sermon* with the word *message* in the bulletin are facing a gap between pulpit and pew that cannot be spanned by mere vocabulary.

The study presented in this chapter indicates that laity come to the Bible expecting to be affected by what they encounter there. Such an effect is not simply, or even primarily, cognitive; it tends to be more aesthetic or emotional. Clergy, however, tend to be more interested in identifying and communicating messages in the text that are both relevant to the present congregation and compatible with the original intent of the author. Given this reality, two types of problems may occur: (1) laity who are prone to construing meaning as effect may respond to the text in idiosyncratic ways; and (2) clergy who are inclined to equate meaning with message may end up answering questions that no one was asking.

The bridge over this gap may involve a compromise solution: we can preach sermons that attempt to affect people (thus meeting the interest of laity) but that do so in certain ways (thus avoiding speculative or idiosyncratic concerns). We may preach for effect in ways that remain relevant to the current needs of the congregation and that are compatible with the original intent of the author. Look again at the responses to Luke 3:3-17 presented on pages 84–89. You probably regard some of these responses as spurious or silly—they may be based on simple misunderstandings of the passage or they may be produced by strained or ridiculous impositions of modern concerns. Anyone who knew what the author meant to communicate in telling this story would not be affected this way. But is that true for *all* of the responses? My guess is that you will find a few responses—not just one, but a few—that you will regard as appropriate or even profound. Luke would be pleased to know his story had this kind of effect on people some nineteen hundred years after it was written. And you would be pleased to have people in your congregation respond this way. Your task as preacher, then, is to proclaim the story in a way that encourages *certain* effects.

In the first chapter of this book, I spoke of "polyvalence within parameters" (see page 4). Polyvalence is a reality. Bible stories mean different things to different people and, whether we like it or not, our sermons are going to mean different things to different people. If we simply read Luke 3:3-17 out loud, people might respond to the text in *all* of the ways recorded above. Preaching on a text allows us the opportunity to set some parameters: if we view preaching as "the performance of scripture," we will recognize the sermon as an opportunity to re-present the text in ways that will encourage some effects over others. We can explain what might be misunderstood, emphasize what we regard as key elements, encourage empathy with one or another character, and basically allow the explicit or implicit story to work for us in generating the kinds of effects its author would have wanted it to produce. To know what those might be, we still need to do our homework: traditional, author-oriented exegesis that helps us determine whether what we hope to accomplish in the sermon is not only relevant to the current context but also appropriate to a historical and contextual understanding of the text that is being proclaimed.

Laity tend to equate the meaning of a text or a sermon with their reaction to it, that is, with what it "does to them." This proclivity could be problematic in any number of ways: it may be naive and narcissistic, or it may imply some superficial preference for sentiment over substance. But there is also a positive potential that we would be foolish to ignore. The basic idea that Scripture is meaningful to the extent that it affects those who encounter it is compatible with a biblical concept of "the Word of God" as an active force that does things to people. When we preach the Word of God, we will craft and perform sermons that have the capacity to do what the biblical text would do, to affect people in ways that the text would affect them.

Ultimately, the task of the preacher is simply to turn the Word of God loose. We don't just talk about the Word of God—we turn it loose. The Word of God creates, heals, judges, redeems. It is not just a message. A sermon is not a message either. It is a release. We turn the Word of God loose to do what the Word of God does.